Ockham Explained

D1523030

IDEAS EXPLAINED™

Daoism Explained, Hans-Georg Moeller

Frege Explained, Joan Weiner

Luhmann Explained, Hans-Georg Moeller

Heidegger Explained, Graham Harman

Atheism Explained, David Ramsay Steele

Sartre Explained, David Detmer

Ockham Explained, Rondo Keele

IN PREPARATION

Rawls Explained, Paul Voice

Phenomenology Explained, David Detmer

Deleuze and Guattari Explained, Rohit Dalvi

Ockham Explained

From Razor to Rebellion

RONDO KEELE

OPEN COURT
Chicago and La Salle, Illinois

Volume 7 in the Ideas Explained™ Series

To order books from Open Court, call toll-free 1-800-815-2280,
or visit our website at www.opencourtbooks.com.

Open Court Publishing Company is a division of Carus Publishing Company.

First printing 2010

Printed and bound in the United States of America.

Library of Congress Cataloging-in-Publication Data

Keele, Rondo, 1968-
    Ockham explained : razor to rebellion / Rondo Keele.
       p. cm. — (Ideas explained series ; v. 7)
    Includes bibliographical references (p.   ) and index.
    ISBN 978-0-8126-9650-9 (trade paper : alk. paper)
       1. William, of Ockham, ca. 1285-ca 1349. 2. Philosophers, Medieval—Biography.
    3. Philosophy, Medieval. I. Title.
    B765.O34K44 2010
    189'.4—dc22

                                                          2009044750

For Gala, and for Sadeem

Contents

Acknowledgments

My thanks to Paul Spade, for introducing me to Ockham's philosophy; to Graham Harman, for suggesting I get involved with the Ideas Explained series in the first place; and to Lisa Keele, for patient proofreading and excellent advice on earlier drafts of this book.

1

Student, Teacher, Thief, Exile

WORTHY BEGINNER—INVINCIBLE DOCTOR

On 26th May, 1328, under the cover of night, a group of figures moves in darkness, preparing for a long journey. Their apartments in the old episcopal palace of Avignon (in what is now France) are otherwise quiet and still. Among the items in their small bundles is a small metal object, shaped like a chess piece but elaborately carved on the bottom. This is the official seal of the Franciscan Order, necessary for the Order to conduct its official business. These men are going to steal it, and take it with them as they slip out of the compound. But they are not simple thieves, in fact they are all Franciscans themselves, escaping into exile, and one of them, Friar Michael, is the Minister General of the Order.

The Franciscan Order had become by then a powerful phenomenon in Western Europe, though just over one hundred years old, and this little theft would not only cause some disruption, it would also be a highly symbolic act. In doing this they defied the will of their host at the palace, Pope John XXII, around whom a storm had gathered in Avignon, a doctrinal controversy that pitted the power of the Papacy against the Franciscan Order.

It seems some Franciscans felt they should not own any property, not even as a group, in imitation of the poverty of Jesus, and this meant that the title to their lands and buildings must be held for them by someone else. Who better to do this than the Pope? The implication was not lost on Pope John XXII that the Franciscans, more than the Pope, were living in line with the example of the Gospels. Pope John could not agree to this arrangement, and told the Franciscans that they should rather render unto Caesar for themselves.

The most outstanding of the Franciscan fugitives, a forty-year-old Englishman named William, was preparing to go on the lam with the seal for a simple reason: he had examined for himself the arguments of John XXII, the evidence adduced by the Pontiff for his point of view on the poverty controversy, and had decided that John's arguments weren't very good; hence, *this Pope was wrong.* Not only was the Pope wrong, but he was being stubborn about his error, in spite of the overwhelming evidence brought against his position. But to persist in error thus is the very definition of heresy, and so it follows that *this Pope was a heretic.* Moreover, our English friar, who was also one of the greatest logicians of his day, finished the syllogism and concluded that since no true Pope would fall into heresy, it follows immediately that *John XXII was no true Pope.* That the Franciscan Order should not fall under the sway of a false Pope, our hero undertook with his fellows to spirit the seal out of Avignon. Without the seal, the Franciscans who remained behind could not be forced to conduct the business of the Order in line with Pope John XXII's wishes, since without the seal no changes to Franciscan practice could be stamped and so made official.

William of Ockham and his companions finally did make it out of town, across the mountains into Italy, and eventually out of Italy even, further north and east than the Pope could easily reach. But John XXII was not amused. This was far worse than when a guest walks off with a bit of silverware.

Logic, defiance, and piety—on these shoals wrecked one of the most promising careers in intellectual history, for, after Avignon, William would never again return west to native England: never return to London, where he once lectured brilliantly on the deepest philosophical controversies of his day; never return to Oxford, where he had been trying to finish a theology degree before his novel approach to theology and the currents of the poverty controversy caught him; never return to the village of Ockham, where he was born. From a distance he would continue the fight against this Pope and, after John XXII died, against the Papacy as a whole, concerning the proper place of the church in political spheres, and the limits of papal power generally. William Ockham would finally die in Munich, and for the final twenty years of life his whole intellectual power was bent on the problems of power and authority, church and state, prince and pope.

This book is designed to explain this great philosophical personality and some of the details of his most original achievements, within the framework of his eventful and controversial life.

Modern people have known for some years that Ockham was one of the three most important European philosophers of the late Middle Ages (along with Thomas Aquinas, who died in 1274, and John Duns Scotus, who died in 1308). He was very original, provocative, and, I think, admirable in his approach to knowledge, reason, and philosophy. However much I (and you) may agree or disagree with his views, they are fun and interesting to discover. As with any important intellectual figure, it remains controversial just who Ockham was intellectually, what he really thought, and how he influenced subsequent philosophy. Some people claim, and not without reason, that Ockham invented the western idea of church-state separation. Some people style him the first modern philosopher, or an analytic philosopher out of his time, or the man who brought the harmonious medieval union of faith and reason to an end in Europe. Some think him a champion of the scientific approach to life. Some claim he was practically a skeptic.

This book will explain Ockham's philosophy in a neutral way; you can make up your own mind about these controversies. Still, I will frame the book around what I believe is the most significant single element of Ockham's philosophical views, and which is the key that unlocks the mysteries and controversies of his ideas. The key is this: Ockham was an excellent logician. That is, his philosophical center of gravity was the proper use of language in thinking and reasoning through philosophical arguments.

As we go along you will see how this fact about Ockham colors all his opinions. His skill and ability with logic lead him to two ideas that are fixed-points in all his thinking:

1. Many philosophers are too simple-minded when they do their metaphysics (when they argue about what must be real) based on *the nature of language*. A simplistic picture of the function of language leads to absurd metaphysical conclusions. We must be more subtle about language.

2. Many philosophers are overly optimistic about the quality of their arguments in metaphysics and theology, and so as a result they overstate *the power of human reason*. We must be more realistic about such things.

Behind both these ideas lies a certain cast of mind, which is, I think, the key to his philosophical personality. It is just this: Ockham had *very, very high standards of evidence*, and in general he thought that, when judged by these standards, much of the philosophy of his day was sloppy, puffed-up, speculative, and misguided.

Some Basic Dates in Ockham's Life

Since this book takes Ockham's life as its frame, there is no need to give a biography in advance; the book as a whole is biography and introduction to his philosophy all in one. Still it is worthwhile to give here some sketch of dates and main events, which I have broken up into 'Important Dates' and 'Odds and Ends', so that you can begin to construct a mental framework for the trajectory of his life.

IMPORTANT DATES

Below are some things we know about Ockham with reasonable certainty:

1285–1288

Born in the village of Ockham, just southwest of London.

Before the age of 14

He joins the Franciscan Order, a religious group dedicated to preaching, and observing strict vows of poverty.

1306

Ordained a subdeacon in London, some time in his late teens or early twenties.

1317

He begins lecturing on theology at Oxford. These lectures are a required exercise for all students of theology who want to become masters of theology. Many of the ideas we will examine in Chapters 3–6 come from these lectures.

1324, Spring

Before he finishes his studies, some time in his late thirties, Ockham is summoned to the court of Pope John XXII to answer certain questions about his views. Essentially, he is investigated for heresy. While there he gets caught up in the poverty controversy between the Franciscan Order and the Pope.

26th May 1328

The escape from Avignon, described at the beginning of this chapter.

1347

Dies in Munich, around age sixty.

INTERESTING ODDS AND ENDS

- Because he had to leave Oxford before his training was finished, he never completed his degree. Basically, he never quite finished what we would today call the 'Ph.D.' Possibly for this reason his colleagues gave him the Latin nickname *Venerabilis Inceptor*—which means 'worthy beginner'. But the name can also mean 'great innovator', a testament to his originality. His other Latin nickname is *Doctor Invincibilis*, which means just what you think it does.

- Ockham was a formidable and popular debater. He took part in medieval philosophical debate-contests called 'quodlibets', and was seldom lost for words. He did seven such debates that we know of, addressing about 170 controversial questions therein.

- Ockham wrote almost all of his philosophical and theological works between 1317 and 1324, enough to fill nineteen large volumes today. He earned his fame in logic and metaphysics, but after 1324 he never wrote another substantial work on philosophy, logic, or theology—nothing but political theory for the last twenty years of his life.

- After the escape from Avignon, on the way to Germany, Ockham once had occasion to hide in the city of Tournai. John XXII sent a letter threatening to burn down Tournai unless the citizens turned him in. They didn't, but the Pope did not carry through his threat.

An Outline of This Book

These facts and dates will form the skeleton of the book. We will follow Ockham's career and thought chronologically, each chapter corresponding to an important period in his life, and to some of the philosophy relevant to that period. The date ranges that head each chapter overlap (for instance, Chapter 2: 1302–1317, Chapter 3: 1317–1319) because, as everyone who went to school knows, the academic year does not coincide with the calendar year. *Ockham Explained* is intended to be read as a continuous narrative, with biographical discussion at the beginning and the end of each chapter; hence, biographically, each chapter builds on those before. I invite the reader to read the chapters in the order they appear, and so to follow the thread of Ockham's life all the way through to the end. However, the philosophical discussions in each chapter could certainly be read independently, except that Chapter 2 gives background useful throughout the whole book, and Chapters 3, 4, and 5 form a unit—an explanation of his core views on metaphysics and logic. A summary of the chapters:

CHAPTER 2. The Young Man (Birth–1302): Aristotle, the Church, and the Medieval University.

> This chapter sets out, non-technically and briefly, those elements of Aristotelian philosophy, medieval theology, and university life which are necessary to understand anything at all about Ockham's life and ideas.

CHAPTER 3. The Student (1302–1317): Ockham's Early Philosophy of Language.

> This chapter fills in some more detail about his intellectual milieu (in particular his teachers and early opponents at Oxford), and puts the reader straightaway into the central philosophical issue that animates his early thinking and forms the hard kernel of all else: the connection between language and reality. The chapter ends in transition to Chapter 4, foreshadowing the one-two punch with which he would attack his opponents: connotation theory and his famous razor.

CHAPTER 4. The Teacher at Oxford (1317–1319): Ockham's Connotation Theory.

> Ockham had made quite a splash as a student, and, as he moved into the early duties of his teaching career at Oxford,

he continued to refine his opposition to the metaphysics of his day, and to consolidate his opinions on language and reality into a coherent approach we call 'connotation theory' today.

CHAPTER 5. The Teacher Attacked (1319–1321): Razors and Anti-Razors.

Nearly everyone has heard of Ockham's razor—'Do not multiply entities beyond necessity'—but few people understand the principle to any great depth, and it is often used today to support reasoning that Ockham himself might have found suspect. As Ockham's teaching career continued, he met determined opposition, especially from a slightly younger fellow friar named Walter Chatton (died in 1343–44), who sat in on Ockham's lectures as a student and raised some difficult questions against him. Chatton developed a kind of anti-razor to combat Ockham's razor. This chapter examines the real meaning and content of Ockham's razor against the background of his dispute with Walter Chatton.

CHAPTER 6. The Teacher Responds (1321–1323): Physics and Motion.

Since some of Ockham's immediate Oxford opponents (including Chatton) were still living with him, probably in a Franciscan House in England, his response to them was swift, and characteristically thorough. This chapter both (1) gives a worked example of how Ockham applied connotation theory and the razor together against their metaphysics, with a look at his theory of motion, and (2) uses this example to expand into a general discussion of his views on physics, which were developed in commentaries on Aristotle, written in this period.

CHAPTER 7. The Teacher Interrupted (1323–1328): Ockham's Showdown with the Pope.

Ockham was no less controversial in his theories on the human intellect and will, with their pragmatic daughter-disciplines, epistemology and ethics. We segue into this aspect of his thought by looking at the interruption (forever as it turned out) of his theological career. During his last years in England,

and just as he was summoned to the papal court in Avignon on suspicion of heresy, he produced his mature thought on the topics mentioned above, which were ascendant in academic debates at Oxford and London at the time. His shift away from language, logic, and metaphysics had begun.

Chapter 8. The Exile in Munich (1328–1347): Ockham's Political Theory.

Cleared of the original charge of heresy at Avignon, Ockham nevertheless became embroiled in the question of how papal wealth could be squared with the Christian virtue of poverty. Having decided (and publicly declared!) that the contemporary pope, John XXII, held heretical views on the subject, and so was no true pope at all, Ockham was forced to flee the west into the on-again, off-again Holy Roman Empire, centered in modern Germany. Political theory, including church-state relations, dominate his thinking and writing for the remainder of his life.

Chapter 9. Afterword: Ockham's Influence and Legacy.

To this day, Ockham is sometimes celebrated as a champion of modernity, sometimes reviled as the destroyer of Aquinas's earlier faith-reason synthesis, and sometimes either celebrated or reviled, depending on one's point of view, as an early instigator of the Reformation. In this last chapter I discuss his influence (surprisingly weak, initially, in England, but strong in Paris; later reversed) and I consider some of the popular modern myths surrounding him, in light of everything we have learned in previous chapters.

This structure is not meant to suggest an extremely tight connection between the periods of Ockham's life in the chapter titles and the subject matter being explained in the chapters; for example, Ockham wrote on physics at other periods of his career besides 1321–1323. But with this qualifier in mind the reader can assume a general correspondence of ideas and life-stages: for example, several of his most important works on physics were done in 1322, and his work on political theory, which is explained at the end of the book, really did come at the end of his life as well.

The Fate of the Seal

Michael and Ockham were not really stealing the seal, since Michael was the minister general, and so was its lawful steward. But they did not have permission to leave Avignon, and their clear intent in taking it was to prevent John XXII from giving Franciscan imprimatur to his own views on poverty. It was for this act that the Pope eventually excommunicated them both, in the summer of 1328. And of course stealing the seal did not ultimately stop John XXII from imposing some unpalatable changes on the Franciscan Order, even if this action did slow him down for a while. Eventually a new seal was made, and was given to a new minister general, one more amenable to the Pope's view than Michael of Cesena had been. Although some of the Franciscans who went into exile in 1328 gave up the cause fairly quickly under the pressure of excommunication, and returned to obedience, Ockham and Michael fought on. But in order to learn whether or not they held out in the long run, and how the whole affair ended, I'm afraid you'll have to simply have to wait until Chapter 9.

2

The Young Man (Birth–1302)

ARISTOTLE, THE CHURCH, AND THE MEDIEVAL UNIVERSITY

The late medieval period in Europe was a time of crusades, knights, battles, disease, disruption, and rapid religious and economic development. But it was not a time of good biography. We have little information on the early lives of most medieval philosophers, and William Ockham is no exception; among other factors, the dearth of general literacy meant that there are no historical records about the lives of most people, especially their early lives.

We know about Ockham mostly from the trajectory of his ecclesiastical career and his mature ideas, together with the controversies these things generated. Fortunately, good research has been done on the general state of education in England during this period of time, enough for us to paint a general picture of young William's intellectual world.

He was born sometime between 1285 and 1288, probably closer to the later date. The place of his birth, Ockham, was at that time a tiny village in the open hill-country of county Surrey, about thirty-five miles south-west of London—and it remains a small village to this day, except now it is just off the A3 motorway, about half an hour from the busy capital. It was not so well connected to the outside world in the late thirteenth century. Thirty five miles is a two-day journey by foot, maybe one by horse.

Young Ockham's world was small, and opportunities for travel from the village and for learning inside it were quite limited. We don't know whether Ockham was robust or sickly, handsome or plain, tall or short. We do have a sketch that purports to show him as an adult, a line drawing in a Cambridge University manuscript which dates to about 1341. This drawing shows a thin man, slight

11

of build, with delicate features; his smile is peaceful and slightly whimsical. How accurate this drawing is cannot be determined, however, and indeed, it may have been made many years after Ockham was dead, and thus be no real likeness at all. At home with his family he would have spoken what we today call Middle-English (think *Canterbury Tales*) or perhaps French. His social status is not known, but it is not likely that it was very high, for Ockham Village was not a site of any special political, economic, or geographical importance.

A boy of talent would be lucky to escape such a place, whatever its rural charms, in order to develop his gifts. But for this possibility to become reality William Ockham would need to learn to read, speak, and write Latin, the language of education, research, and administration throughout Western Europe. He may have picked up some Latin from his local parish priest, but his first real break came sometime before the age of fourteen: he joined, or rather was 'offered' to the Franciscan Order, and in exchange for obedience and service, was educated by the Order in Latin, simple Aristotelian logic, basic theology, and some natural science.

Some of this schooling may have happened in London, but at any rate it did not occur in Ockham, for the Franciscans did not have a convent anywhere in Surrey. Wherever he first learned his grammar and Bible, it is quite certain that William was studying in London with the Franciscans by 1306, at around the age of eighteen, but most likely he began with them there several years earlier. His hope must have been that, after another few years of this basic training, the preparation would give him a chance for advanced study of theology, either at Oxford or Paris, or at one of the Franciscan's own theology institutes, called *studia* (singular *studium*). He eventually studied and taught theology for a time at Oxford, and it is probable that in fact he studied and taught in London as he got older. But this gets us too far ahead of the story.

To follow Ockham's mature thinking in later chapters, and to understand his philosophical personality, it seems clear that we must follow along for ourselves the path of his intellectual development from boyhood, and take a conspectus of those things that he learned in grammar school (except, of course, Latin!). As may be gathered from the story so far, the three social and cultural factors at the foundation of his intellectual life are those listed in the chapter title: Aristotle, the Church, and the Medieval University.

Some explanation of these three elements are therefore necessary to understand anything about Ockham's later philosophy.

In the remainder of this chapter we shall discuss them in this order: first, the incredibly influential writings of the ancient Greek philosopher Aristotle, especially his work on logic, physics, metaphysics (= theories about ultimate reality), and ethics, which writings had, 150 years earlier, made a kind of comeback in the Latin West after many years of dormancy; second, the Western, Latin church, with its long tradition of literacy, its well-developed theology, its powerful and well-organized hierarchy of deacons, priests, bishops, and its orders of teaching friars, like the Franciscans; and finally, the Western-European university, which was a relatively new phenomenon in the late thirteenth century when Ockham was born.

Aristotle

All of Ockham's philosophy, and indeed, all the philosophy done in Europe during Ockham's lifetime, has an Aristotelian cast to it. Even thinkers who consciously rejected Aristotle's ideas were indebted to him for many basic concepts of philosophy, and Aristotelian logic was universally regarded as the correct basis of the science of reasoning. Ockham viewed himself as foremost a theologian, not an interpreter of Aristotle (who died in 322 B.C.), but Ockham clearly regarded Aristotelian philosophy as important to the rational science of theology, since Aristotle was the most important systematizer of what could be known on the basis of reason. Indeed, many of Ockham's complaints about his contemporary philosopher-theologians amounted to the charge that they had misunderstood Aristotle and even abused his ideas to form elaborate and needlessly ornate accounts of reality. Ockham commented extensively on several of Aristotle's most important works, especially the *Physics*, which discusses motion, change, and cosmology. Aristotle's ideas will therefore come up throughout all parts of this book, so it is important from the outset to fix in the reader's mind certain basic Aristotelian tenets. What follows is a purpose-built explanation of Aristotle, reflecting the kind of Aristotelianism that would have been taught to young William, not necessarily a faithful reading of Aristotle's texts themselves.

Form

Perhaps the most influential contribution of Aristotle to the history of ideas is his notion of *intelligible form*. Plato (died 347 B.C.), once Aristotle's teacher, was among the first philosophers to recognize this powerful idea, which Aristotle then developed in a certain direction.

When Plato reflected on the similarities between numerically distinct things in this changing world of the senses he felt that the cause of those similarities must be something existing in its own right. For example, think of the way the multiplicity of distinct individual people nevertheless all share the common traits of our species, or, imagine rows of seats in a theater, in which distinct individual seats are nevertheless exactly similar in color, shape, size and function, in a word, are exactly the same in *form*. These seemingly abstract similarities, Plato thought, must somehow be real. So too, if Socrates and Xenophon are both actually morally excellent human beings, both just and fair, say, then the ideal, formal cause of their similarity must be a real thing—a Form (Greek *eidos* or *idea*); we could call it 'Justice Itself'. And in general, if it is objectively true that Socrates has a property *p* and that Xenophon the same property *p*, then this structural fact has as its cause a formal entity in objective reality, the Form 'P-itself', which entity we can consider with the mind but not with the senses.

In fact Plato thought that the Form 'Justice', like any perfect Form, must exist apart, separated from Socrates and Xenophon, who are imperfect, changing, sensible substances. This Justice—not the justice in each of the men, but the one, unified Justice itself, the single source of their several justices—must in fact be more real than Socrates and Xenophon, since it is the unchanging basis of the intelligible structural feature 'justice' present in these physical men. And indeed, whatever is intelligible about 'the particulars'—about each of the sensible objects of our world—its color, size, relations with other objects, moral qualities, and so forth—all these properties, multiplied in countless instances in different individuals, must each have a single source in a single intelligible, formal reality that underlies this multiplicity.

Plato was convinced that these Forms exist in a completely different way and even in a completely different realm from the particulars, because the former can only be what they are; the Just

Itself must always be just, since it is the very standard of justice. Socrates, by contrast, may be now just but later unjust. Thus, for Plato the realm of Forms is the realm of what is ultimately real, the realm of Being, while the many individual particulars reside in the shadowy reality of mere becoming.

Aristotle famously agreed with Plato's basic idea of intelligible form. However, he insisted that there could not be two worlds, one of Forms, where the source of intelligibility resides, perfect and unchanging, and another where the effects of intelligibility rage, waxing and waning. Aristotle reasoned that if intelligible forms explain the intelligibility of the many, particular, individual sensible objects of this world, then intelligible forms must be denizens of this world whose intelligibility they cause. In fact, intelligible forms are not these grand 'separated Forms' at all, but rather 'immanent forms'—internal metaphysical ingredients of the very objects whose structure they cause and explain. If Socrates and Xenophon are just it is because of a formal cause, justice, but this formal cause is inside Socrates and inside Xenophon somehow, part of their makeup. How else could it be a cause of the justice in Socrates and in Xenophon?

Aristotle also reversed Plato's view of the relative importance of these two kinds of beings, forms and particular individuals. Plato thought of the Forms as independent and unchanging, and so most real; Aristotle noted that it is for the sake of the particulars that forms have their effects, so it is rather the individual particulars, such as Socrates, Xenophon, a seat in a theater, or this book in your hands, which are truly independent and central, and so most real. He calls such individuals *primary substances*, to reflect how they form the rock-bottom basic level of reality in his view. Today we often use the interchangeable term *individual substance* to remind ourselves that for Aristotle, individuals, not general forms, are metaphysically primary.

Essence, Accident, Genus, Species

Aristotle's theory of intelligible form differs from Plato's not only on the importance and 'location' of forms, it also takes a more sophisticated view of the varieties of intelligible forms. Since forms explain the intelligible features of things, we must invoke them to explain all kinds of intelligible change. For example, if Socrates was pale, and after a day in the sun is now tanned, then previously he was affected by the form of pale, and now by the form of tan. Underneath it all he is still really the same basic Socrates, still a human being, a rational animal. However, even that more basic fact can change too; when Socrates dies, those uniquely human capacities of reason and understanding, in short his human nature, will be gone, and this change is not trivial and reversible, but is rather more substantive and permanent. The first kind of (relatively trivial) change, from pale to tan, Aristotle called *accidental*; the second, (more profound) kind, from human being to non-human being, he called *substantial*. These two types of intelligible change correspond to two types of intelligible form as well. Since every individual substance is an individual of a certain fundamental type (as Aristotle put it, a *this something*), we can focus on that thing's *substantial form*, which is connected with that individual's basic type or *essence*, the what-it-is-to-be that kind of thing. On the other hand, since every individual also has many fluctuating non-essential characteristics, e.g., color, location in space, proximity to other objects, and so on, accidental change forces us to recognize the existence of *accidental forms* as well. Sometimes referred to simply as *accidents*, from Latin 'accidere' = 'to happen to occur', accidental forms are forms that things happen to have, but which they could lack and still be the kind of thing they are.

Substantial forms explain what an individual substance is most fundamentally; we refer to substantial forms when we answer the question 'What is it?' Imagine pointing to Socrates and asking 'What is it?' The most specific, accurate way to answer would be to name his species, 'human being', but also correct would be the higher categories 'animal', 'living being', or even 'material being'. Aristotle noted that the answers to the question 'What is it?', at least in reference to organic beings, often take the form of genus and species words, since these words seem to capture most fundamentally the right answer to the question. 'Human being' is a *species*, while 'animal', 'living being' and each of the other, higher categories words in our example is a *genus* (plural *genera*). The point is that substantial forms, which are fundamental and capture the essences of things, are to be associated with genus and species.

By contrast, since accidental forms explain more superficially what an individual substance is, we refer to accidental forms when we answer the question 'What is it like?' The answers to this question, Aristotle noted, are of bewildering variety: for example we could remark of Socrates that he is 'pale', 'snub-nosed', 'two meters tall', 'wearing sandals', 'in front of Plato's house', etc. Aristotle tried to give an account of these various ways of answering the question 'What is it like?' in his book *Categories*. Strange to say, this account served as the basis for an enormous amount of controversy in the Middle Ages, in which controversy Ockham became deeply involved. Consequently, Aristotle's remarks in the *Categories*, which we today refer to as *the doctrine of the ten categories*, is one of the most important ideas for understanding Ockham's battles with his contemporaries.

Language, the Ten Categories, and Real Definition

In Chapter 4 of his brief logical tract *Categories*, Aristotle gave this dark and compact formula, seemingly a list of ten categories:

> Of things said without any combination, each signifies either substance or quantity or qualification or a relative or where or when or being-in-a-position or having or doing or being-affected. (J.L. Ackrill's translation in *The Complete Works of Aristotle*, p. 4)

Aristotle then 'explained' himself by listing examples for each of the ten categories he mentions. I restate his list below. The order and wording are slightly different—more on that later—and I have added my own examples, similar in spirit to Aristotle's own examples from the *Categories*:

(i)   substance—for example, Socrates and Xenophon

(ii)   quality—for example, pale, cold, just

(iii)   quantity—for example, two meters tall, half as much as yesterday

(iv)   relation—for example, the servant of, in front of

(v)   time—for example, yesterday, Friday March 31st, 2006

(vi)   place—for example, in the Louvre, near New York

(vii)   position—for example, upside down, tilted left

(viii) having—for example, wearing shoes, wearing a coat

(ix)   doing an action (= action)—for example, heating, breaking

(x)   receiving an action (= passion)—for example, being heated, being broken

This opaque passage is one of the most important texts for the history of medieval philosophy. But what in the world does it mean?

First, we should reread the quotation above and note some important basic points. The phrase "things said without any combination" just means 'individual words, standing alone', as opposed to words grouped into sentences. For example, here are some words standing alone, 'figs, time, boil', and here are the same words grouped into a sentence, 'There's no time to boil these figs.' So, we should understand Aristotle as follows: 'All words standing alone signify either substance or quantity or quality or relation or time or place or position or having or doing or being done to.'

Given this, some things about the passage start to become clear, while others remain hazy. First, it's clear that this is a classification of extra-linguistic reality, not merely a grammatical typology; it is not merely a classification of ten different types of *words*. He wrote "Of things said without any combination, each *signifies* either substance or quantity . . .," and we must admit that words normally signify objects in the external world, not other words. It is also clear, once we look carefully, that everything falling under category (i) is an individual substance existing in reality, that is, category (i) includes things such as Socrates, Xenophon, the book in your hand, and so forth—while things in categories (ii)–(x) are accidental modifications of such individuals—being pale, being two meters tall, and so on. However, while it is clear that Aristotle's categories refer to the world outside of language—that his categories are categories of non-linguistic things words signify—it is also clear that this passage implies a connection between world and language, between the actual Greek human being Socrates and the word 'Socrates', for example. This is evident, if you look carefully: 'Of things said (*language*) some signify substance (*a certain kind of reality in the world*) or quantity (*another kind of reality in the world*) . . .' Hence, Aristotle has in mind some connection between words and non-linguistic realities. But which realities? And what connection? Here the interpretation opens up considerably, and here too is where Ockham and his contemporaries later disagreed.

Let's focus on the nine accidental categories (ii)–(x) for a moment. What did Aristotle mean to imply with this world/language connection? Here are some possibilities for what he could have meant:

1. that accidental forms can be thought of in nine categories, and by the way, here they are,

or,

2. that there is a nine-fold typology of accidental beings, and here it is,

or rather more conservatively,

3. that there seem to be these nine ways that accidental form-words signify things, but we can make no assumptions about what the things they signify are or what they are like,

or even more conservatively still,

4. here are nine categories which are useful for thinking about all the ways we can answer the question 'What is it like?' (while pointing to some piece of non-linguistic reality, say, pale Socrates; likewise for his height or his location).

Interpretations 1 and 2 strongly suggest that not only are 'accident words' (such as 'pale' or 'two meters tall') divided in this nine-fold way, but that the nine-fold linguistic division corresponds directly to a nine-fold division in types of accidental beings. These interpretations imply or assume that *there are in fact* nine kinds of accidents in the world corresponding to the nine accidental categories listed, suggesting that a plethora of distinct accidental forms really exists and can be categorized, not unlike the way a plethora of birds really exists and can be categorized. For example, category (vi) *place*, is a category of accidental form, so according to interpretations 1 and 2, we should think of the examples associated with that category, e.g., the accidental forms <u>in the Louvre</u> and <u>near New York</u>, as actual *things*, as real in their own way as the *Mona Lisa* or Connecticut. Moreover, 1 and 2 also suggest that if I am in the Louvre, and if it is therefore true to point to me and ask 'What is it like?' and to answer 'in the Louvre', then this is because I have the accidental form <u>in the Louvre</u> as part of me in some sense. In short, interpretations 1 and 2 lead very naturally to the idea that Aristotle's categories are categories of real things existing in the world, even though some of those beings are quite normal and everyday (Socrates) while others are strange (<u>in the Louvre</u>).

Interpretations 3 and 4 by contrast are much more conservative, and don't lead to any such easy one-to-one identification. They suggest rather that while language and reality are connected, the nature of the connection may be obscure, and we cannot necessarily reason from a nine-fold division in language to a nine-fold division in reality. According to these interpretations, it is as if in the *Categories* Aristotle were only saying 'words signifying things in the world do their job according to this ten-fold typology, one of substance, nine of accident,' or 'here is a heuristic for organizing substance-words and accidental-form-words'. However, these conservative interpretations leave open the question whether or not the typology on the linguistic side implies anything about the correct typology in the world, that is, on the ontological side. As we shall see, having absorbed his Aristotle well as a boy, the grown-up Ockham spent much of his time trying to convince his colleagues by various ingenious means that interpretations such as 1 and 2 are dangerous, unreasonable and send philosophy into nonsense, and that interpretations such as 3 and 4 are more rational.

Another, related controversy about the deep connection between language and the world was inspired by Aristotle's notion of substantial form and essence: if the essence of an individual substance such as Socrates is the what-it-is-to-be a thing of Socrates's kind (that is, the what-it-is-to-be-human), then this essence, <u>humanity</u>, must have a counterpart in language, a definition, if you like, which tells what the essence is. After Aristotle it became standard to say, for example, that the definition of 'human being', that is, the linguistic formulation of the essence <u>humanity</u>, is just 'rational animal'. Because the definition 'rational animal' explains the essence of a human being, indicating what it really is, deep down, such a definition is called a *real definition*. Any individual substance is a real thing, and so has an essence, and so has a real definition, according to Aristotle. Ockham's opponents later made much of this seemingly innocuous idea, extending it and using it to argue for the existence of many things Ockham found dubious, and he felt obliged, as he did with the doctrine of the ten categories, to reign in these metaphysical pretensions.

Cognition, Universals, and the Soul

Finally, as an end to Aristotelian preliminaries, we must mention Aristotle's basic views of how we perceive and understand objects. Ockham and Aristotle were of one mind in their basic attitudes toward human cognition: all knowledge, they believed, arises from experience.

Perhaps this is too strong for Ockham; he recognized that some things we rightly believe come to us, not from direct experience, but by reasoning (say, in mathematics), or by revelation (he is a theologian, after all). Aristotle too recognized the role of reason in knowledge. Nevertheless Aristotle, and Ockham in his turn, were what we call *empiricists*, people who privilege the role of sensory experience above all else in the production of what is properly called 'knowledge'.

Aristotle made a sharp distinction between sensation and intellection, the two cognitive processes which he attributed to the mind or soul (Greek *psyche*) of the human animal. Sensation, he said, is of the particular. Say, for example, I see a magnolia tree in the middle distance; what I see is a *this something*, this magnolia tree. Since it is an individual substance, we could even give it a proper name; 'Maggie' seems appropriate. Aristotle would say that when I see Maggie Magnolia, it is because Maggie somehow interacts with my organs of sight across the distance between us, and on this basis I assemble, as it were, a *sense concept* of Maggie which is peculiar to her. This is how sensation happens for any animal, not only for human beings; the *sensitive soul* constructs a sense concept of the particular individuals it senses. By contrast intellection, or understanding, which is unique to human beings, is of the universal. In the human soul some power is able to strip away what is particular about Maggie, and so to remove or *abstract* from the particular sense-concept 'Maggie Magnolia' the general, universal *intellectual concept* 'magnolia tree'. When I think in general terms about magnolia trees using my intellectual concept 'magnolia tree', I am thinking, not of Maggie Magnolia in particular, nor of Margaret Magnolia either, nor of any particular magnolia tree. Rather, with the universal intellectual concept I think of magnolias generally, insofar as they are magnolia trees; just magnolia nature, if you will.

So much was accepted by most philosophers in the Middle Ages. However, several interesting issues arise immediately out of all this. My particular sense concept of Maggie Magnolia is *of* a particular thing, because it is caused by that particular thing, that is, by Maggie. Aristotle and most mediaeval philosophers were thus *direct realists*, believing that we sense, usually directly and unproblematically, the external world around us. (Contrast this with Descartes's *Meditations*, and the tendency of modern philosophy after him endlessly to fuss over the problem of the external world.) Ockham followed Aristotle in this direct realist view, and in the idea that individual things have essences or natures, and he saw no real problems with this outlook.

Later philosophers would sometimes take another step beyond this simple realism, and would claim that, as it is in sensation, so it is in intellection, and therefore, since my universal intellectual concept of magnolia trees is *of* a universal thing, it is *caused by* a universal thing—presumably the universal essence *magnolia tree*. This suggests that, when I have universal intellectual knowledge about the nature of things, for instance when I know that *magnolia trees are broadleaf evergreens*, the object of my knowledge must be a universal essence, and hence *universal essences are real parts of the external world, and are the objects of all general knowledge*. Since these universal essences, also called 'common natures' or simply 'universals' (such as *magnolia tree*) are, well, universal, and since individual instances of them (Maggie) are particular, universals and individuals must be distinct types of reality. This suggests that universal essences have some real status on their own, and are in some way distinguishable from any particular individuals they instantiate. So, it seems, the essence or nature *magnolia tree* in fact exists as an ingredient of individual magnolia trees, although it has a kind of being apart from Maggie and Margaret and all other particular individual magnolias trees.

Ockham would have completely rejected the view that there is such a thing as the universal essence *magnolia tree* that exists apart from Maggie and Margaret Magnolia. He spared no energy in rejecting the view that universal essences are the objects of general knowledge and in showing instead that the connection between language and the world is not so simple; you can't necessarily reason from the existence of universal *concepts* in thought and language to universal *realities* in the world that those concepts are about. Ockham accepted the basic Aristotelian ideas outlined here: form (substantial and accidental); essence, natures, genus and species; general, universal concepts; and even the idea of ten categories. All are useful and all have a place in a rational understanding of the nature of reality. But people who say we can reason easily from any of these doctrines to grand theories filled with a zoo of invisible metaphysical beings are making too much of Aristotle.

The Church

Ockham was offered to the Franciscans as a boy, and he remained in the Order all his life. This entails that after studying his Aristotle, Ockham would have learned the basics of theology from the educational system of the Franciscans, which was separate but not fundamentally distinct from the basic educational system of his society at large. From his Franciscan schooling, Ockham absorbed his basic outlook on God, the human good, and the ultimate nature of reality. Hence Christianity was the foundation of his intellectual outlook. Even when he was arguing metaphysics or logic with his contemporaries, his ideas reflect the Christian culture of medieval England, not only in doctrine, but even in trivial examples. Names, places and sample-sentences used to illustrate his non-religious logical points were apt to be about religious subjects, just as today examples are apt to be drawn from popular music or films. Even though Christianity is a familiar phenomenon in the English-speaking world, because the philosophical underpinnings of the religion were so much a part of Ockham's world-view, some of the central theological tenets of this Middle-Eastern monotheism must be explicitly put before the reader at the outset.

Background, Books, and Bishops

Christianity began as a movement within Judaism, based on the life and teachings of the Jewish charismatic Jesus, and swiftly spread around the central and eastern Mediterranean, eventually becoming the official religion of the Roman Empire. It was subject to a number of fairly early crises over doctrine, resulting in numerous schisms throughout its long history. For example, the Egyptian church, administered out of Alexandria, split from the Greek church in Constantinople in the mid-fifth century A.D., in part over the issue of whether Jesus, whom Christians regard as the unique incarnation of God, has two substantial forms, one human, one divine, or rather simply has one human/divine substantial form. Taking the latter view at the council of Chalcedon (A.D. 451), the Church of Alexandria fell out with the Greek church, which preferred the first formula. Even here, one thousand years before Ockham, we see the influence of the Aristotelian idea of substantial form on theological questions!

Another major split was sealed in 1054, when the remaining Greek Christians in the Eastern Empire and the Western, Roman Church broke from each other. The Western Church, Latin speaking, centered in Western Europe, and calling itself 'catholic' (meaning 'universal'), was the instantiation of Christianity into which Ockham was born and to which he paid allegiance all his life, even when he became a reformer in later years. Henceforth we will refer to this branch simply as 'medieval Catholicism'.

In Ockham's day, medieval Catholicism took as its textual basis the Vulgate Bible, a fifth-century A.D. Latin translation by Saint Jerome based on a collection of older Hebrew and Greek manuscripts. Also very important for Ockham and his contemporaries were the following groups of texts:

1. *Patristic literature.* The texts of early Christian writers of the ancient world, especially saints such as Augustine, Bishop of Hippo (d. 430), had great prestige and status. Patristic literature includes many genres, for example original theological and philosophical texts, but also commentaries (for example, on certain books of the Bible), and even polemical writings (for example, catalogues of heresies).

2. *Non-patristic theological writings.* Any medieval philosopher-theologian will obviously be interested in the writings of other, more contemporary philosopher-theologians, and

Ockham read lots of texts by medieval thinkers as well. Most important for us is a book by twelfth-century theologian Peter Lombard (d. 1160), usually called the *Sentences* (= 'the judgments'), in which he repeatedly (a) states a theological problem, then (b) summarizes the patristic literature on the topic, and finally (c) gives his own judgment on the issue (hence the book's title). During Ockham's lifetime all theology 'graduate students' in Western Europe were required to teach a one- to two-year theology course using the *Sentences* as a textbook. The lectures they prepared to read to their students were often published afterwards, and those that have survived are among the best sources we have for medieval philosophy. Today we call these published lectures '*Sentences* commentaries'. Ockham has at least two different *Sentences* commentaries, but not all parts of all versions survived. Many of the ideas discussed in Chapters 3–6 come from Ockham's *Sentences* commentaries.

3. *Papal bulls.* When official orthodox doctrine needed to be set out, the pope would proclaim the official position in a formal document called a bull. As we will see in Chapter 8, sometimes these documents had political and philosophical implications.

The medieval Catholic Church famously developed many administrative and spiritual problems in the high Middle Ages. The selling of indulgences, giving of benefices as political favors, and scandals in the papacy are the most notorious examples of conditions leading to the deterioration of the Church's prestige. An important internal revitalization of this powerful institution occurred in the early thirteenth century, when Saints Dominic and Francis established new religious institutions of preachers, who were charged to go about in the world teaching the tenets of Christianity to the infidels and lapsed Christians. Each of their respective orders, the Dominicans and the Franciscans, eventually became sponsors of very powerful academic unions at the newly established universities of Paris and Oxford. The fact that Ockham belonged to a reform-minded, academically powerful religious order will have serious ramifications for his career, as we will see in Chapters 7 and 8.

Top Ten List: Some Philosophically Important Christian Doctrines

Below I indicate some doctrinal themes of Ockham's religion which figure importantly in his philosophy. I do not claim that these tenets are the most important themes in Christianity, or that all Christians believe them, but only that they are most important for our purposes. Ockham would have believed all of these things. He would not have considered them as random hypotheses among others in a marketplace of ideas, and in fact 1–3 would be for him mysteries that reason can aid only in clarifying, but cannot necessarily prove, and indeed, no such proof is needed. The remaining items are propositions he would not doubt, but which he would be willing to investigate further using reason. These are also doctrines with specifically philosophical content, which were subject to fierce interpretive battles in Ockham's day. In short, items 4–10 are where a lot of philosophical action will be in later chapters.

1. *The incarnation.* Every Christian believes, and it is diagnostic of Christian belief, that God somehow became a human being for a time in the person of Jesus. This belief is usually literal for the Christian. It is not that God inspired Jesus, or guided him minutely; no. God became man. Christians believe that this was necessary to correct human nature so that human beings can be finally redeemed.

2. *Trinitarianism.* Medieval catholicism held that God, although one, is somehow three at the same time; the three are called the Father, the Son (Jesus Christ), and the Holy Spirit. This is not an easy idea to explain or defend, and seems to conflict with item 8 below.

3. *The Bible.* The Bible is a divinely revealed book, not a human product. However, the book is written in language, and covers profound subjects; hence it needs to be understood and interpreted.

4. *The doctrine of creation,* namely that *God freely created everything besides himself ex nihilo.* This has enormous philosophical consequences. One cannot properly understand Ockham's razor (Chapter 5) without first understanding this doctrine. Take it in pieces:

(a) *God freely created* . . . This means that the cosmos, the intelligible order, the universe, is a product, which came into being in time or with time, and that its very existence is due to God. Moreover, this creative act was not necessary. God could have done otherwise. Consequently every existing thing besides God might not have existed: in other words, it is all contingent.

(b) . . . *everything besides himself* . . . God is the creator as in 4a above for every existing thing, except himself. God did not produce himself, nor did anything else; God is not self-produced, but *un*produced.

(c) . . . *ex nihilo.* This Latin phrase means 'from nothing'. That is, God did not work from a pre-existing, eternal substance, and fashion *it* into the universe. God is not merely a craftsman, as in Plato's *Timaeus.* Before the creation there was *only* God.

5. *Divine omnipotence.* God is held to be capable of doing anything that can be done, or to have power without limit. Ockham interprets this to mean that God can bring about anything, unless bringing that thing about would involve a contradiction. So, for example, although God can't make a stone so big that he can't lift it, this is no reflection on the power of God. The property so-big-it-can't-be-lifted-by-God cannot be realized, not because God lacks power to realize it, but because the bringing about of the property itself is impossible; after all, the description of this stone contains a contradiction inside it, since 'so-big-it-can't-be-lifted-by-God' refers to a being without physical limits (God) as having physical limits. But then God cannot make such a stone, not because of problems in him, but because of problems *in the stone so described.* If such a stone *could* be made at all (which we now see it cannot be), then God could make it.

6. *Divine command morality.* God is the source of the moral law. That is, what God forbids is not morally permitted, what God allows is morally permitted, and what God requires is morally obliged. The very meaning of the concept 'moral' is given by God's commands, prohibitions, and allowances.

7. *The human good/predestination.* The very best possible thing for a human being is to be judged worthy of heaven after death, and to be rewarded there with the *beatific vision*, a kind of 'seeing' or experience of God himself. However, it is God himself who decides who gets this privilege; God does not owe it to anyone.

8. *Divine metaphysical simplicity.* God is metaphysically simple and wholly internally unified. There is no composition in God, not form and matter, not potency and act, not thought and deed. Again, this may conflict with 2 above.

9. *God has will and intellect.* Not like we do, but nevertheless, the God of Christianity is a personal God. As per 8 above, this will and intellect must be really one in some sense.

10. *Angels.* There are beings, neither human nor divine, which are closer to God than we are. They do not have bodies—indeed they are immaterial—but they do have intellect and will; that is, they are persons. Their pin-head dancing is, of course, legend. However, strange as it may sound, angels were often a fascinating test-case for certain philosophical theories.

The Church and Aristotle

Here is a useful, succinct and not entirely false sketch of medieval intellectual history in Western Europe. In the beginning there was only Aristotle. Then there was the Church but no Aristotle, and the breadth of Greek learning generally, was in fact lost. In the early twelfth century the Latin West got back into Greek learning because Greek text got back into Latin. Finally, from the early twelfth century until the end of the Middle Ages we have a sometimes uneasy mixture of the Church and Aristotle.

Now here is a slightly more refined version of this same sketch. From around the sixth century A.D. to around 1120 or so, the Latin West had access to the following major books of Aristotle and Plato in general circulation in Latin:

1. Aristotle: *De interpretatione, Categories.* These works are on logic and language. Note they did not have his most impor-

tant works, such as the *Metaphysics*, *Ethics*, *Physics*, or *De anima*.

2. Plato: half of the *Timaeus*.

In other words, they didn't have much. And they couldn't read Greek either, so they couldn't get at the originals. (The Arab world was doing much better at this time; they read Greek and so had access to all the great stuff.) Beginning in around 1120, and continuing until around 1250, the works of the ancients came into Latin translation, and with them learning was revitalized in the Latin world. The proximity of Muslim and Christian kingdoms in Spain may have played some role in this transmission.

Given this history, it is easy to see why Latin speakers were really overcome when they got ahold of Aristotle's *Metaphysics*, *Physics*, and other works. At first they did not understand what was going on. They originally relied on Muslim commentators like Ibn Rushd (whom they simply called 'The Commentator' out of respect, as if he were the only one in the world!); later less so. In the chaos of this amalgamation of the new translations of Aristotle and Plato at least two trends occurred, both of which are understandable, given all these events:

1. *Unification.* Some of the things Aristotle says flatly contradict Christian theology. For example, Aristotle seemed to think that the universe is eternal. But this contradicts the doctrine of creation (item 4 above). Aristotle and Plato laid great stress on reason as a source of authority, while the Church privileged ecclesiastical authority and sacred texts (3 above). But it's hard to put Greek philosophy down once you start with it. Could Greek learning and Christian dogma be unified? Could reason and faith be reconciled? Some thinkers, like Aquinas, believed strongly that such a unification was possible, and attempted to carry one out.

2. *Going a little nuts with the new Aristotle.* Just like a kid with a new toy, or congress with a new budget, the Latin intellectuals couldn't leave it alone; they couldn't stop playing with their Aristotle. They even extended his ideas in certain ways, one or two of which were hinted at above.

Ockham's reaction to both these trends was generally negative. He was not very impressed with some of the unification projects he saw in the work of other theologians, nor was he at all impressed with some of the extensions of Aristotle that he encountered in the work of his philosophical contemporaries. However, his views are nuanced and complicated on both fronts; he was neither a fideist nor anti-Aristotelian. More than anything he seems simply to have had very high standards when it comes to argumentation and evidence. He objected, not to the unification of faith and reason, but to the facile unification of faith and reason; not to the extension and application of Aristotle's ideas, but to simple-minded and fruitless extensions of them. Most of the fruitless extensions to which he applied his withering logical powers were dreamt up by fellow theology students and teachers at Oxford, London, and Paris; so we turn now to a brief description of the university systems that produced him and his opponents.

Medieval Universities, *Studia*, and Theology Study

The most important basic distinctions for understanding Ockham's place in the medieval institutions of higher learning are (1) the difference between *arts faculties* and *higher faculties*, and (2) the difference between *regular and mendicant theologians* on the one hand, and *secular theologians* on the other.

1. ARTS FACULTIES AND HIGHER FACULTIES

There was no compulsory formal education in fourteenth-century England; only the fortunate could take in the advanced learning of the Western tradition through formal schooling. The fortunate did not include any young women, nor most young men. Those few young men who did have this chance began their education at around age seven. First, for a year or two, they studied the basics of the Latin language; next, some went on to study Latin grammar, simple logic, and the Bible, for six to ten years. This two-stage basic training was completed on average around the age of fourteen, when most of those who were able to move on began their 'undergraduate training' (so to speak) in the *arts faculty*. The teachers of the arts faculty were a group of older students who had been through arts training themselves, and also *masters*, who had completed their training and dedicated themselves to teaching arts. The curriculum comprised language sciences (grammar, logic, and rhetoric, the so-called *trivium*) and also physical science, mathematics, and humanities (music, astronomy, arithmetic, and geometry, the so-called *quadrivium*). Arts training could take around seven to nine years to complete.

After a student finished with basic education and arts training, on average at the age of twenty-one, he could then go on to one of the *higher faculties*, what we might call graduate/professional study today. There were three higher faculties in the Middle Ages: theology, law, and medicine. These courses of instruction were quite long, and could take the student into his mid-thirties or beyond. Hence, a very normal course of study for a fourteen-year old who wanted to become a theologian would be to go to a university town that had an arts faculty and a theology faculty (Oxford and Paris had the most famous such universities), and there go through arts, then through theology. Theology training, like undergraduate plus graduate training in humanities today, took as much as fourteen years; the average age of a theology lecturer at Oxford in the fourteenth century was thirty-five. The highest award and office one could hold at the end of this training, the equivalent of our Ph.D., was the 'doctor of theology'.

2. REGULAR THEOLOGIANS, MENDICANT THEOLOGIANS, AND SECULAR THEOLOGIANS

Not everyone became a theologian through this route. In particular, those who belonged to any religious order that demanded its members follow a rule (Latin *regula*) were called *regulars*, and their course of study had to fall in line with the rule they followed, for example, it had to be consistent with the vows of obedience to superiors that were usually a part of those rules. This often entailed following somewhat different courses of early study, which were given in special schools attached to the religious houses where the brothers actually lived. Religious orders included the mendicant orders, such as the Franciscans; hence all Franciscan theologians in this period were required by the Order to do the equivalent of arts training at a school run by and for Franciscans; modern scholars call these general-education schools *studia generalia* (singular *studium generale*). In effect, these students got a university education outside the university. They learned the same things that arts students did, and could also go on to study theology, for example, but when they did go on they were considered *mendicant theologians*, meaning that they had trained with a mendicant order as 'undergraduates'. Obviously, given these definitions, all mendicant theologians were regular theologians.

Those who pursued the other route, discussed in 1 above, in other words those who did their 'undergraduate training' in arts before going on to theology, were called *secular theologians* by contrast. This phrase sounds like an oxymoron to the modern ear, but it simply refers to those theologians who were not regulars, that is, were not associated with a religious order, and who therefore did arts as undergraduates. A close modern analogy might be the difference between home-schooled students and public educated students in the United States. Both groups are supposed to learn the same things, and both can continue their higher education in the same places, but the former group is kept apart for early training. The key idea is 'parallel but separate'. Mendicant theology students often studied their discipline at universities (such as Oxford) just as seculars did, but, in keeping with the 'parallel but separate' theme, the Franciscans also ran their own advanced schools which taught the particular curriculum of theology, and which were therefore called a *studia particularia theologiae*.

Theology training was by far the most rigorous of all the higher faculties, more rigorous than law or medicine. Theology students were required to write sermons, to give lecture commentaries on the Bible and on the *Sentences*, and also to practice defending, attacking, and resolving very abstract disputes on the nature of God and man. Not everyone who started finished, but those who did were the most educated persons in their society.

Several points emerge from all of these distinctions. First, as a Franciscan, Ockham was a mendicant theologian, and so did not study in arts; instead he did *studium generale* training outside Oxford, most likely in London. Second, he studied in the higher faculty of theology for several important, formative years at Oxford University, and at the Franciscan *studium particulare theologiae* at Oxford, but he also studied theology at the smaller *studium particulare theologiae* in London. It seems he was moving back and forth, taking classes and eventually giving lectures in both places, according to the wishes of his superiors and the needs of the order.

Third, even when he was at Oxford, studying with a mixture of mendicant and secular theologians, he lived, taught, and interacted intellectually mostly with fellow mendicant theologians, and in particular with fellow Franciscans.

The upshot is just this: despite his original and far-reaching philosophical mind, Ockham's intellectual world was, in certain important ways, very small. Intense, certainly, but still small. In saying this we do not mean to suggest his training was inadequate or second-rate; on the contrary, no doubt it was excellent. But until his adulthood Ockham had little exposure to the wider world, and he showed in his early writings no concern with the problems of the world—of politics and ethics—topics that fate would force the mature man to consider against his will, while his career with the church crumbled around him.

Language, Truth, and Logic

For all the gaps in our knowledge of his early life, it seems clear that the young William Ockham adroitly ascended the educational ladder we have just described. After learning his ABCs and his Latin, he took liberal arts lessons at the Franciscan *studium generale* in London, learning the basic Aristotle sketched above; he then began his theology studies at a Franciscan *studium particulare* (in London or Oxford, we're not sure which), and was eventually singled out from among many others to continue on in theology at Oxford, the most precious educational opportunity that his social world could possibly give him. But that takes us too far ahead of the story.

Just now, we find Ockham, around the age of fourteen, beginning to attend advanced lectures in Aristotelian philosophy in a Christian context at the *studium* in London. What he learned there was also learned by countless other boys before and after, but, to judge from the results, one subject made a more profound impression on this boy than any other subject, and would become the cornerstone for all his later metaphysics—namely, logic. For Ockham, it begins with the nature of language and truth.

3

The Student (1302–1317)

OCKHAM'S EARLY PHILOSOPHY OF LANGUAGE

This phase of Ockham's life includes his 'undergraduate years', in a sense. As we have seen, for a medieval theology student these times started much earlier and lasted longer than they do for modern students, but for Ockham, this formative stage included all of what we call high school and even some of what we regard as graduate or professional school.

How large a life-change the move to London was for him, around the age of fourteen, is uncertain. Had he ever even been out of Surrey before? What is clear is that, as he attended lectures on more advanced philosophy topics, probably at the custodial school associated with the London convent, he was deeply impressed with the subject of logic, which, at this time, was naturally connected to what we now call 'semantics'. We cannot know for certain who were his teachers in London, but we do know that many important English Franciscans of that time came through there on business, educational and otherwise. Possibly Ockham even had occasion to meet John Duns Scotus, the greatest English philosopher of the time.

It is even more difficult to pin down who his friends and colleagues might have been. Of the three Oxonians who were later important interlocutors and opponents of his ideas—Richard Campsall (active in the first half of the fourteenth century), Walter Burley (died 1344), and Walter Chatton—only Chatton could possibly have been among his *early* colleagues. Campsall was an older contemporary, who was with Ockham only later, at Oxford, but he was a secular theologian anyway, and so would have gone to different schools to prepare for Oxford. Similar remarks apply to

Walter Burley, an older secular who taught as a master in the arts faculty at Oxford from 1301 to 1310, for most of which time Ockham would have been in London, and anyway, as a mendicant Ockham did not study in arts. Chatton, although a Franciscan who followed the same kind of career path as Ockham into the theology program at Oxford, was born in the north, almost in Scotland, and most likely received his early education there as well. He and Ockham did not catch up with each other until around 1317. By the early 1320s they had lived and studied together for several intense years, and Chatton had become Ockham's greatest critic. But this influence on Ockham was late, relative to the period we are examining now. Consequently we won't meet Chatton properly until Chapter 5, when we examine Ockham's razor.

The most basic analytical concept in all of Ockham's thinking about language and truth—and hence to all this thinking about metaphysics and ontology—is the idea of a *term*. (What a term is I shall explain shortly.) The rich semantic theories based on properties of terms extended back centuries in the Latin tradition of logic. Ockham would have studied these theories when he learned advanced logic during this phase of his life. But Ockham was not some kind of young logic genius who revolutionized medieval logic while a student in London. Rather, we should say that the theory of terms was absolutely formative on his philosophical personality, and that he was innovative, clever, and original in his later application of these theories to metaphysics and ontology. The purpose of this chapter is to follow out this important concept so that this later application to metaphysics makes sense.

Since we don't have a copy of the textbook that Ockham was using in London as he began his studies of logic and semantics, we must have recourse to the next best thing: namely, the introductory logic textbook that Ockham *himself* wrote as an advanced (nearly finished) theology student in the early 1320s. So while the view of logic we will find in this chapter is derived from one of his mature texts, we will confine ourselves to the kinds of basic issues he would have studied as a young man, before 1317. The book I have in mind has come to be known as the *Summa logicae*, which means something like 'The Complete Book of Logic'. This modestly-titled tome is enormous, and clearly had an important rhetorical function in addition to its pedagogical function as an introduction to logic. For in it Ockham not only talked about the usual topics covered in logic books of his day, he also editorialized on what he regarded as the foolish excesses of contemporary metaphysics. Consequently, we will have occasion to visit this text more than once; it will help us understand both his early and mid-career philosophy.

A final word to the reader before turning to Ockham's views on language. This chapter is about language and logic, and since these things were so fundamental to Ockham, the ideas in this chapter are fundamental to everything that follows. No background is assumed for this section of the book, and every attempt is made to avoid being overly technical. But logic was (and is) a technical subject, and mastering some of Ockham's technical vocabulary is essential. There are three points the reader may wish to keep in mind concerning all this.

1. The next section, 'What Is a Term?', is a brief, easygoing introduction to some important basic ideas in medieval logic; those very familiar with modern logic may be tempted to skip this section, and this will do little harm, but in the section after that we quickly get into topics unique to late medieval logic and semantic theory, and this section should not be skipped for similar reasons.

2. The payoff to the reader for learning about Ockham's logic will be immediate, because the lessons we learn about term logic here will be applied *immediately* in Chapter 4 to the problems of metaphysics. As you read Chapter 3, note especially the Ockhamist conclusions I place in boldface type in this chapter; each one of them finds immediate application in the next chapter.

3. To aid the reader and make things fun, the chapter includes a 'quiz' so you can check your comprehension. Moreover, all of the technical terms in this chapter are briefly defined in the Glossary at the end of the book for easy reference.

What Is a Term?

To answer this question we must first briefly discuss propositions and arguments. When we reason well we move reliably from certain pieces of information, called *premises*, to another piece of information, called a *conclusion*. In general we call a movement of reasoning, whether it is done well or not, an *argument*. An example of an argument, with the conclusion in italics:

> If knowledge is possible then there must be a part of reality that is an immutable standard. No part of reality is an immutable standard; *therefore, knowledge is impossible.*

The chunks of information in an argument, whether they are a premise or a conclusion, are called *propositions*. The argument above contains three propositions, but only two sentences. Broken down by proposition, the parts of the argument are these:

(1) If knowledge is possible then there must be a part of reality that is an immutable standard.

(2) No part of reality is an immutable standard.

(3) *Knowledge is impossible.*

Some arguments are long and complicated, with many premises. However, following Aristotle, who first invented the type of logic we are discussing here, medieval logicians tended to try wherever possible to analyze reasoning into a series of simple argument forms called a *categorical syllogisms*. Here are some examples of categorical syllogisms (Argument II is invalid, the rest are valid; more on this topic in a bit):

Argument I

No Greek poet was eccentric.

All geniuses are eccentric.

No Greek poet was a genius.

Argument II

All students are politically active.

Some Spaniards are politically active.

Some Spaniard is a student.

Argument III

Man is a rational creature.

No rational creature despises liberty.

No man despises liberty.

Argument IV

'Snow is white' is a true sentence.

Every true sentence is worth knowing.

'Snow is white' is worth knowing.

Argument V

No circle is rectilinear.

This shape is a circle.

This shape is not rectilinear.

Notice that all these arguments have two premises. So do all categorical syllogisms. There are other things they have in common as well. One is that while the propositions in each argument are about various topics, each one is a *categorical proposition*—a proposition of one of the following eight forms:

(1) Universal affirmative (A-form):   All S is P.

(2) Universal negative (E-form):   No S is P.

(3) Particular affirmative (I-form):   Some S is P.

(4) Particular negative (O-form):   Some S is not P.

(5) Indefinite affirmative: S is P.

(6) Indefinite negative: S is not P.

(7) Singular affirmative: This S is P.

(8) Singular negative: This S is not P.

If you study forms (1)–(4) above, looking for common patterns, you will begin to see that these categorical propositions have four parts, or as we say, four *terms*:

Q S c P = Quantifier Subject copula (either positive+, or negative-) Predicate

For example: <u>All</u> <u>birds</u> <u>are</u> <u>animals</u>. <u>Some</u> <u>cars</u> <u>are not</u> <u>usable.</u>
  Q   S   c+   P   Q   S   c-   P

The indefinites and singulars, (5)–(8), all lack a quantifier term, of course, but they still have a subject term, a copula, and a predicate term:

<u>Term logic</u> <u>is</u> <u>fascinating</u>
    S   c+   P

The subject term and predicate term of a categorical proposition Ockham called the *extremes* of the proposition. It is because the extremes of a categorical proposition are usually category words like 'desk' or 'birds' that these propositions are called 'categorical'.

Now we get to the whole point of all this. Categorical syllogisms are composed of categorical propositions, and categorical propositions are composed of terms. Moreover, as I said above, Argument II is invalid, and so worthless, but the others are valid. How can we know this? One way would be to talk through the arguments, and try to find a counterexample to the invalid one. But this is too imprecise. In fact, we know that Argument II is invalid because from the science of logic we know that *any argument whose terms are arranged as the terms in Argument II are arranged is invalid*. Indeed, any argument of the form:

All A are B

<u>Some C is B</u>

Some C is A

is invalid. What makes it invalid is the arrangement of the terms. In particular it is invalid because term B, called the 'middle term', is not governed by either negation or universality (there is a rule which says that the middle term of a valid categorical syllogism must be so governed). Likewise, the arrangement of the terms in Argument I makes Argument I, and any argument like it, valid. Indeed, for Ockham, this applies to other kinds of arguments, not just categorical syllogisms. Nearly all of basic syllogistic logic is simply the study of the properties of terms, and of rules formulated for how to correctly use terms in reasoning, for example, rules for their correct *arrangement* into propositions and syllogisms. We even call the logic of Ockham and people like him *term logic*. So we come to the definition of 'term' that will serve us throughout:

A *term* is a logically significant constituent element of a proposition.

Terms are those pieces of a proposition such that, if we know their properties and behavior, we can thereby systematically separate correct reasoning from incorrect reasoning; that is, knowing about terms allows us to do logic. Note that another common word for 'term' in Ockham's vocabulary is 'name', from Latin *nomen*. So Ockham will sometimes say 'connotative name' for 'connotative term', for example. But a term is not just a word; 'term' is a logical, not a grammatical concept. For example, the subject term in 'Term logic is fascinating' is *term logic*; one term, but two words.

It remains in this chapter to study the different classifications or divisions Ockham gives to terms. Ockham believes that by applying only a handful of such distinctions he can take down much of the metaphysics of his day.

Divisions of Terms

When Ockham began to write his *Summa logicae* as an older man, he started out his exposition just as it would have been presented to him as a young man, just as we have followed here only more briefly, by defining the idea of a term. But he then set out a number of basic divisions between terms. Again, these distinctions were not unique to him, but were just the same as those he learned as a younger man at the London *studium*. The first distinction Ockham made defines three levels of language generally; that is, it defines three levels of language (called 'written', 'spoken' and 'mental') both for individual terms and for whole propositions. The distinction was common coin in his day; hints of it appear as far back as Aristotle and Augustine.

Written language. We make shapes with pencil, chalk, etc. on paper or another appropriate substance, and the shapes represent sounds. Thus, we have a written, visual system of communication, which can transmit understanding from one person to another. The shapes of the systems differ, for example, the written symbols ω, Ж, կ, ڡ ,ছ,ઓ, and are all from different writing systems. At some point in the history of humanity, people made up or borrowed such written letter-shapes and word-shapes to stand for spoken words and sounds; spoken language is of course earlier and more basic. There exist, therefore, written letters, written words, or as Ockham prefers when discussing logic, *written terms,* and also *written propositions.* Notice, this level of language depends directly upon spoken language, which is the next level.

Spoken language. We open the holes on the front of our faces and racket comes out. Some of this racket is meaningful speech, an aural system of communication which can transmit understanding from person to person. Again, the sounds of spoken languages differ; for example, Arabic speakers often have trouble distinguishing the sounds that go with the English letters 'b' and 'p', and English speakers have trouble with the sound of the famous Arabic ع 'ain'. So there are spoken sounds, which when significant form *spoken terms,* which form *spoken propositions.* The spoken level is more basic than the written level; writing is a later invention than speech. Is spoken language the ultimate level? No, says Ockham, there is a deeper level of language: that of thought itself.

Mental language. It is easy to get the wrong idea about mental language. It is not simply the words you can sometimes 'hear in your head' when, for example, you think in German or in English. That phenomenon is simply imagining spoken language to yourself; it is no more actual language than imagining running is actual running. Rather, mental language is the language of thought and of reasoning, the language your mind works in, of which you are not even directly aware. Ockham believed there are *mental terms* and *mental propositions* in this language, universal to all human beings.

I want to adopt a notational convention to make these levels easier to discuss. Instead of writing, for example, 'the *spoken term* "bat"', or 'the *written term* "faint"', which is cumbersome, and which involves lots of quotation marks, instead I will write a little subscript, '$_s$' for spoken, '$_w$' for written, and '$_m$' for mental, so you know which level we're talking about. For example, the spoken term bat will be written as bat$_s$, and the mental term faint will be written as faint$_m$.

There are many important differences between mental language and the other two levels:

1. Mental language is the basis of spoken language, which is in turn the basis for written language. But mental language is not based on any deeper level. Or, as Ockham might put it: cat$_w$ is *subordinated to* cat$_s$ which is *subordinated to* cat$_m$, but cat$_m$ is not subordinated to anything else:

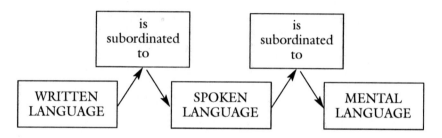

2. While there is but one mental language for all human beings, obviously spoken and written languages vary considerably. There is some evidence for this view:

(a) *Translation.* The reason why Latin 'salus' and English 'safety' *mean the same thing* is that they are both expressions of *the very same mental term*, or as we usually say, the same *concept*. Translation from one human language, spoken or written, is possible because human beings share one common mental language.

(b) *Synonymy and equivocation.* Within languages we have spoken terms with the same meaning, like quake$_s$ and shake$_s$, or ethics$_s$ and morality$_s$. How to explain this? In each case we have two spoken signs which are subordinated to the same concept, or mental term. Similarly, spoken English words like bank$_s$ and bank$_s$, which have two distinct meanings, get explained in the opposite way: the same spoken sign is subordinated to two mental terms:

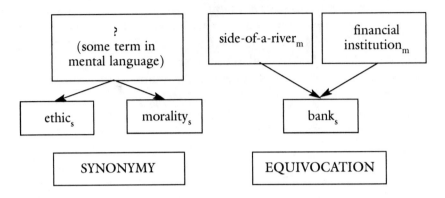

3. Another important fact is that mental terms naturally connect with the things they signify (= the things they cause you to think of), whereas spoken and written terms connect with the world and with their mental counterparts only conventionally. That is, we make up the term fig$_s$; there is no reason why the sound fig$_s$ should pick out that tasty fruit. Why not bligblug$_s$? If everyone starts calling figs bligblugs then they are bligblugs. It's up to us. Similarly with written terms. But mental terms do not signify *ad placitum* (at our pleasure), as Ockham puts it, but *naturaliter*, that is, naturally. We don't make mental language up, we are born with it.

4. Finally, there is nothing fancy in mental language. There are no irregular verbs, no alternate spellings (colour and color), no grammatical gender. Only what is relevant to truth, falsity, and reasoning appears in mental language.

Beyond this doctrine of the three-fold levels of terms and propositions, there are many ways systematically to approach the variety of terms. Broadly speaking, young Ockham learned to think about terms in three ways as a student: (1) concerning what terms do; we might say, the natural *behavior* of terms, (2) concerning the particular uses we put terms to; we might say, the *applications* of terms, and finally (3) concerning the simple varieties or species of terms; we might say, the different *types* of terms. To illustrate how this works, think of a similar systematic approach to *birds*. A person wanting to learn all she could about birds might look at their natural behavior (such as courtship dances), at their uses, (such as falconry), and at their basic types (for example, different genera and species). These modes of study would affect each other, certainly, (for instance in falconry we <u>use</u> birds of the <u>genus</u>

accipiter) but it is not the case that one can study just one of these modes and fully understand birds, for there are no necessary connections between the modes (for instance, many birds who are not remotely related in *species*, exhibit similar fishing *behavior*, such as the kingfisher and the pelican).

So too for us, a conspectus of the behavior, uses, and types of terms as taught to young Ockham will help us unlock his philosophy beginning in Chapter 4. Below I talk through the most important divisions of terms. At the end of each section I indicate in bold type the lessons that Ockham drew from this early study, and later applied in metaphysics.

The Behavior of Terms

Two types of natural behavior of terms are of interest to us: *signification* and *supposition*.

SIGNIFICATION

The most basic thing that terms do is to make us think of things. When an English speaker hears the term cat_s something happens in her head; we should say she is put in mind of cats. Or, using the terminology learned so far, we might say that cat_s makes her think of cats by activating cat_m.

Not all terms exhibit this cause-to-think-of behavior, of course. For example, when a literate English speaker reads all_w, he is not necessarily put in mind of any *thing* in particular or in general. As we will see below, all_w is a special type kind of term that affects the signification of other terms, but does not really signify on its own. Even so, it must be admitted that many, many ordinary terms do have this signification function. Notice too, terms exhibit this behavior in isolation; that is, the term cat_s has the power *all by itself* to make me think of cats, it does not have to be in a proposition to have this power.

SUPPOSITION

By contrast, when terms *supposit* they must do so in the context of a proposition, not in isolation, just as birds will exhibit certain behaviors only when in flocks. A term supposits in a proposition when it has truth-sensitive reference for the proposition that contains it. For example, the word cats$_w$ is subordinate to cats$_s$, which is subordinate to cats$_m$, which signifies cats, and hence, when I read cats$_w$, it puts me in mind of cats. But in the context of the true proposition '*Cats* was a popular musical,' I am using the term cats$_w$ very differently from its normal signification; there it refers, not to cats, but to a musical play about cats. In this proposition, the reference of cats$_w$ has changed in a way that makes a difference to truth, because the collection of animals we call cats, although generally popular, are not musicals, and so taken this way the proposition would be false.

People distinguished different kinds of supposition in the Middle Ages, and these theories varied considerably from author to author, but the three-fold outline that Ockham stuck to throughout his whole career was as follows:

1. *Personal supposition.* A term supposits *personally* when it refers to what it normally signifies. For example, the underlined term in the proposition 'A <u>man</u> came to see me yesterday' has personal supposition, because the term 'man' simply refers to exactly the kind of thing the term normally calls to mind, i.e., a male human being. Similarly, the term 'two-lettered words in English' has personal supposition in this proposition: 'Most <u>two-lettered words in English</u> are prepositions.' Contrast this with

2. *Material supposition.* A term supposits *materially* when it (a) refers to its own spoken or written symbol and (b) does *not* refer to what it normally signifies. This is very like the modern philosophical distinction between use and mention. For example, the underlined term in this proposition, '<u>Man</u> has three letters,' clearly has material supposition. The subject term in this proposition, unlike 'A <u>man</u> came to see me yesterday', refers, not to the thing 'man' normally makes you think of, but rather to the three-letter written English word. We might say that the subject of 'A <u>man</u> came to see me yesterday' refers to a male human being, while the subject of '<u>Man</u> has three letters' actually refers to man$_w$. So too there is material supposition when we say 'Hate rhymes with eight'; what we mean is that hate$_s$ sounds like eight$_s$; in this case 'hate' and 'eight' have material supposition.

Notice, given what we have said, in the proposition 'At is a two-lettered word', the subject, *at*, has material supposition, but the predicate, *two-lettered word*, has personal supposition. But note that in 'Two-lettered word is a hyphenated phrase', the underlined term has *material supposition*. In sensible modern English writing we use quotation marks to indicate that a term is in material supposition, thus: 'Two-lettered word' is a hyphenated phrase. Medieval writing systems lacked quotation marks.

3. *Simple supposition.* A term supposits *simply* when it (a) refers to its own mental term, that is, its own term in mental language, and (b) does *not* refer to what it normally signifies. For example, the underlined term in 'Philosophers find political equality elusive' has simple supposition. This proposition does *not* mean that philosophers have trouble finding political equality for themselves in their societies—it does not mean that philosophers are a disenfranchised bunch—it rather means that they find the concept *political equality* an elusive one to pin down and properly analyze. It doesn't follow from this that there is no such thing as political equality existing as an entity in reality, or that there is not; all we mean is that the proposition above does not evidently refer to this entity, even if it exists. Rather, it refers to the concept of this entity, if it exists. Note that in *this* proposition, 'Political equality is often elusive for linguistic minorities', the same term seems to have personal supposition instead.

The Uses of Terms

TERMS OF FIRST IMPOSITION AND SECOND IMPOSITION

Pretend we are cave people with no written language, and not even a spoken language yet. We are human, so we have the same mental language as everyone else. We want to have a way to get each other's attention about the nasty saber-toothed tiger that would like to eat us, but also to let each other know that the deer we want to hunt and eat is nearby. It won't do simply to make a loud noise on each occasion—'Aaargh!'—since the first situation calls for running up a tree and the second for quietly grabbing your spear. We want different sounds for these different situations. And in general, the *first* obvious use of different words is to signify different things in the world that interest us. So, as we begin to *impose* spoken terms on the world, spoken terms which are subordinate to our natural, shared, mental terms, our *first imposition* of such terms is onto things out there in the world such as deer and tigers. Hence, mediaeval philosophers said, *terms of first imposition* are just these firstly imposed terms, such as deer$_s$, tiger$_s$, or run!$_s$. Eventually we can even develop written language and the same thing will apply; for example, deer$_w$ has first imposition.

Later, when we cave people have developed lots and lots of terms of first imposition, we need to teach grammar to our cave children in cave school, and so we need to organize the terms somehow. We notice that deer$_s$ and its counterpart deer$_w$ signify an object (as do tiger$_s$ and tiger$_w$), while run$_s$ and run$_w$, like fly$_s$ and fly$_w$, signify actions instead. It would be nice, wouldn't it, if we could group all the 'object-terms' together and all the 'action-terms' together—but what could we call these two groups? What's needed is a *second* round of naming here, in order to do grammar and bore children. And so some genius *imposes* a name on all the 'object-terms': "Let's call them *nouns$_s$*," she cries, and riding the momentum, she then calls the 'action-terms' *verbs$_s$*. We have now imposed two new terms on our cave language—noun$_s$ and verb$_s$— these are terms of *second imposition,* for obvious reasons: we had to impose the first round of terms in order to have enough of them around to need to be organized by a second round of imposition. At first we were making up words to use to talk about things like deer (first imposition), then later we were making up other words to talk about the first group of words we made up (second impo- sition). These are distinct uses of language, and it will be useful to recognize the difference.

To make the point succinctly but more technically, terms of first imposition are spoken or written signs that signify elements of the non-linguistic world, while terms of second imposition are spoken or written signs that signify spoken or written signs. Ockham also calls terms of second imposition *nomina nominium,* 'names of names'. We could also say that second imposition—names of writ- ten or spoken signs; first imposition—names of things-that-aren't- spoken-or-written-signs.

Do terms of second imposition refer to mental terms? Ockham would say, maybe, if we speak loosely, but strictly speaking terms of second imposition organize only other spoken or written terms; such terms constitute a vocabulary for talking about spoken and written language, not about thoughts. They are the kinds of words you would expect to find in a grammar manual, not so much in a cognitive psychology textbook. From Ockham's perspective the deeper point is that, whatever they refer to, terms of second imposition always *are* spoken or written signs themselves; so $noun_w$ and $noun_s$ are second imposition, but $noun_m$ is not in any sense a term of second imposition (or first imposition, for that matter). *There are no mental terms of any imposition, first or second.* I leave it as an exercise below to say why.

TERMS OF FIRST INTENTION AND SECOND INTENTION

This new distinction, which unfortunately is superficially similar in name to the last one, is really quite different, and applies only to terms of first imposition in the strict sense, that is, only to names of things-that-aren't-spoken-or-written-signs, that is, names of non-linguistic things in the world. If we consider things in the world that aren't spoken or written signs, we notice that some of them exist in the mind, or are *mental*, while some exist outside the mind, or are *extra-mental*. We often call things in the mind *concepts*, or as we have been saying, *mental terms*, and we notice that some words in our spoken and written language seem to refer only to these beings of the mental world. These are terms we use to talk about our minds, essentially. Ockham calls all such first imposition terms of this kind, the kind that refer to the contents of our minds, *second intentions*. The most obvious example of a spoken term of second intention is $concept_s$. But we have also made up other, more specialized terms of second intention. For example, we notice that our concepts of the natural world differ in generality: we have certain concepts in mental language, such as man_m, $donkey_m$, $frog_m$, which all organize things according to kind, but on a low level of generality. We call them 'species'. We also notice that the concepts man_m, $donkey_m$, and $frog_m$ all fall under the concept $animal_m$, a higher level mental term that organizes man_m, $donkey_m$, $frog_m$, and so forth. We call $animal_m$ a 'genus'. Similarly $rock_m$ could be a genus. Consequently, we can say that the corresponding spoken and written terms such as genus$_w$ and species$_w$ name concepts, and so are terms of second intention.

By contrast, some things in the world that aren't spoken or written signs are not mental; in fact most things that aren't spoken or written signs are not mental. When we impose spoken or written names on these objects, those names are said to be *first intentions.* The vast majority of our terms are like this. Examples include man$_s$, animal$_s$ Plato$_w$; each of these spoken or written terms signifies a part of reality that is (1) not a spoken or written sign, and (2) not a concept. Man$_s$ signifies men, and Plato$_w$ signifies the famous philosopher. Both terms signify human beings, which are pieces of non-linguistic, non-conceptual reality. A picture might help:

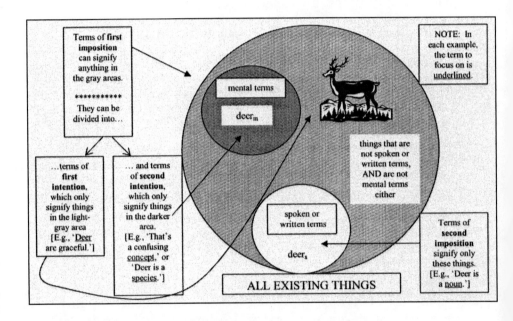

To sum up: sometimes we are talking about spoken or written language, so we use terms of second imposition; usually we're not and so we use terms of first imposition. Suppose we are *not* talking about spoken or written language. At those times we are either talking about mental things, that is, about concepts, using terms of second intention, or else about non-mental things, using terms of first intention. The lesson Ockham carried into later life from all this was that **we must be very careful to distinguish situations**

in which we are talking about language, as against situations when we are talking about non-language, and similarly to distinguish when we are talking about mental things versus non-mental things; in particular, we must be careful to distinguish cases where we are really talking about concepts in subtle ways—cases where we are using terms of first imposition, second intention.

Quiz Time!

We can't very well live young William's school days with him without taking a test. Here we have a (needless to say) optional quiz you can take to see how well you are absorbing all this stuff on terms. An answer key follows on the next page.

Ye Olde Terme Quizze
(questions increase in difficulty)

1. What kind of imposition does the underlined term in each proposition have? If applicable, also say what kind of intention each has.

'Philosophy helps me clarify my <u>ideas</u>'.
'<u>Ideas</u> comes from the Greek ιδεα.
'<u>Ideas</u> has five letters'.

2. What sort of supposition does each of the underlined terms in 1. have? (Remember, your choices are *personal*, *material*, or *simple* supposition.)

3. Suppose you start an internet business and decide to call your company 'Ideas'. Now consider the following proposition:

'I hope <u>Ideas</u> does not go bankrupt.'

Give the imposition, intention, and supposition of this underlined word.

4. Can you say in a single sentence why are there no mental terms of second imposition (or first imposition, for that matter)?

5. Does the term first-imposition$_s$ itself have first imposition? Why or why not?

Answers to Quiz

1. **What kind of imposition does the underlined word in each proposition have? If applicable, also say what kind of intention each has.**

2. **What sort of supposition does each of the under-lined terms in 1. have?**

'Philosophy helps me clarify my <u>ideas</u>.'
first imposition/second intention　　*personal supposition*

'<u>Ideas</u> comes from the Greek ιδεα.'
second imposition　　*material supposition*

'<u>Ideas</u> has five letters.'
second imposition　　*material supposition*

3. **Give the imposition, intention, and supposition, of this underlined word.**

'I hope <u>Ideas</u> does not go bankrupt.'
first imposition/first intention　　*personal supposition*

4. **Can you say in a single sentence why are there no mental terms of second imposition (or first imposition, for that matter)?**

Terms of first or second imposition are 'imposed' or invented, but mental language is natural.

5. **Does the term first-imposition$_s$ itself have first imposition? Why or why not?**

No. The spoken term 'first imposition' signifies spoken or written signs of a certain kind. In particular, terms of first imposition are (a) spoken or written terms that (b) signify non-spoken-or-written-signs. Since the spoken term 'first imposition' signifies spoken or written signs, and a term that is of first imposition signifies non-spoken-or-written-signs, the spoken term 'first imposition' cannot be of first imposition.

Some Types of Terms

CATEGOREMATIC AND SYNCATEGOREMATIC TERMS

A categorematic term is one that signifies, all by itself, in a fixed and regular way. For example, the terms 'man', 'animal', and 'whiteness', each have the power to signify, that is, to make you think of something, all on their own. If I say 'animal', then animal$_s$ causes you to think of animals. A syncategorematic term is one that doesn't signify on its own in a fixed way, but rather changes its signification depending on the words connected with it. For example, the terms 'all', 'every', 'some', and 'only' don't make you think of anything when they are said alone, but put them with categorematic term and—bang!—signification happens. So I say 'some', and the term some$_s$ doesn't do anything for you. But if I say 'some animal' then something happens in your brain. Modern logicians make this same distinction, only they call syncategorematic terms 'logical constants'. Other examples of syncategoremata are: 'or', 'except', 'if', 'unless', and 'ceases'. There are whole books from the thirteenth and fourteenth centuries focused exclusively on syncategorematic terms. This distinction affords an important example of the fact that **some terms are logically significant, in other words significant to truth, without really meaning anything on their own.**

ABSOLUTE VERSUS CONNOTATIVE TERMS

This distinction is less confusing but more elaborate than those we looked at above under "The Uses of Terms," and it is the lynch pin of Ockham's logic-based attack on metaphysics. It applies to all three levels of language: mental, spoken, and written.

Purely *absolute terms* signify entities according to essential form. For example, animal$_m$ is an absolute mental term which signifies animals, like oxen and donkeys, etc. Other examples of absolute terms are 'water', 'heat', and 'sweetness'. The important properties of absolute terms are as follows:

1. Absolute terms apply to all the things they apply to in the same way. Notice that Oscar the ox and Brownie the donkey are both animals in the same way and for the same reason: metaphysically speaking, Oscar is no more an animal

than Brownie. Similarly, the absolute term animal$_s$ signifies animals, and signifies each of them in exactly the same way; that is, animal$_s$ no more signifies Oscar than it does Brownie, because Oscar is an animal in every way that Brownie is, and vice versa. It does not signify Oscar primarily and simply, but Brownie only secondarily. And in general, absolute terms signify all the things they signify in exactly the same way.

2. Absolute terms signify based on essential form. Consequently, absolute terms connect with the real, objective, metaphysical essence or nature of the things they refer to. Absolute terms signify entities which are essentially similar.

3. It follows that (and Ockham actually said that) every absolute term that can be defined has a real definition, i.e., a definition that truly gets at the essence of the thing defined. E.g., the definition of 'human being' is 'rational animal'.

4. Moreover, Ockham insisted, the terms of the real definition of any absolute term each appear on the same grammatical footing. That is, if we don't count the syncategoremata in the definition, the terms in it are all nouns and adjectives in the same grammatical case. For example, the real definition

$$\text{animal} =_{\text{RDF}} \text{animate, sensate substance}$$

does not privilege the adjective 'animate' over the adjective 'sensate'. An animal is not 'an animate thing when it is sensate' as though it were primarily animate and secondarily sensate. No; an animal is animate, and it is sensate, and it is a substance, all three, all equally.

5. Although for Ockham most things only have one essential form, a thing may have several non-equivalent real definitions. This is simply because there are different ways to 'get at' or characterize the essence of a thing. In fact, we may even disagree about the correct real definitions of things. This does not mean that there is no objective answer to our dispute, just that there are non-equivalent ways of characterizing the essential forms of individual substances. For example, consider the absolute term 'angel'. One person may say,

angel = $_{RDF}$ a substance which exists without matter

while another says,

angel = $_{RDF}$ an intellectual, incorruptible substance.

Notice that the terms in these two real definitions are different. They both agree that an angel is a substance, but the second definition mentions the intellectual nature of angels, while the first does not. It is possible that the definitions end up signifying exactly the same reality; indeed, they must if they are truly real definitions of 'angel'. The point is that the definitions are not necessarily equivalent to each other. They are non-trivially different. What's the lesson? **Where absolute terms and real definitions are at stake, metaphysics is at stake, and there can be profound ontological disputes about the entities thus signified.** This claim is one of the single most important parts of Ockham's philosophy.

Connotative terms signify entities grouped by convention alone. They are the opposite of absolute terms in every respect. Examples of connotative terms are 'white', 'similar', and 'intellect'. The important properties of connotative terms:

1. Connotative terms have a complex kind of signification, usually entailing two or more different aspects of meaning. Thus they are the opposite of absolute terms, which signify equally and uniformly. In practice this usually means that each connotative term signifies two or more things unequally, or it signifies one thing primarily, and secondarily the way that thing exists.

   Some examples are needed to clarify this. The connotative term 'similar' *does not* signify all the similar things in the world, the way the absolute term 'animal' signifies all the animals. That is simply not its linguistic job. Indeed, things are similar for different reasons, some because they have similar measure (as a six-foot snake and a six-foot stick), some because they have similar origin (as an Egyptian woman and an Egyptian song), some because they have similar qualities (as a white dog and a white paper). Contrast this with the absolute term 'animal', as above; things are animals all *for the very same reason.*

Consequently, the connotative term 'similar', like any connotative term, is not a 'natural kind term' nor is it the term of a natural metaphysical category.

For a second example, consider the connotative term 'white'. When I correctly identify white in the world, I do so by pointing to an object, an individual substance, which is white. Hence, it is these two elements that the term 'white' signifies: (a) some object, and (b) its manner of existence, that is, the accidental form of <u>whiteness</u> that is a part of it. But these two elements are not equal; it's not as though they are both white the way both Oscar and Brownie are animals. And so this type of connotative term signifies one thing primarily, and secondarily, the way that primary thing exists.

2. As both examples immediately above indicate, connotative terms do not signify based on essential form. Consequently, connotative terms do not connect straightforwardly with the real, objective, metaphysical essence of the things they refer to. Connotative terms that signify two or more entities signify things that are metaphysically connected in only loose, complicated ways, or sometimes not connected deeply at all (as an Egyptian song and an Egyptian woman are both Egyptian).

3. It follows that no connotative term has a real definition; instead, Ockham said, they have *nominal definitions.* A nominal definition of a term is a merely linguistic definition; it simply tells us how the term is used in language, nothing more. For instance, 'white' is basically an abbreviation for the phrase 'something qualified by a whiteness', which is its nominal definition, and 'intellect' abbreviates 'soul, when it has the capacity of understanding'.

4. Although it is clearer to see in the Latin, the terms of a nominal definition of any connotative term appear on different grammatical footing; the fact that they signify one thing primarily and another thing secondarily is grammatically evident, because at least one term in any nominal definition is subordinate to some other term. For example, the nominal definition

white = $_{\text{NDF}}$ something that is qualified by a whiteness privileges the indefinite noun 'something' over the noun 'whiteness', which occurs only in the subordinate, qualifying phrase 'qualified by a whiteness'.[1] A white thing is in fact 'a thing' which then 'has a whiteness'; primarily we are talking about a thing (an individual substance), and secondarily, about its quality, whiteness. Whatever is white is, metaphysically speaking, primarily a thing, and next, has a whiteness.

5. Although a thing can have several distinct nominal definitions, these definitions are all equivalent to one another. This is because nominal definitions tell us how connotative terms function, and the functioning of these terms is usually quite clear upon analysis. There are different ways to 'get at' or characterize the use of a term, but since all language is shared (including mental language), the uses are all basically equivalent if the term is univocal (i.e., not ambiguous). For example, the connotative term 'white'. One person may say:

white = $_{NDF}$ something that is qualified by a whiteness

while another says

white = $_{NDF}$ something having a whiteness.

Notice that the terms in these two nominal definitions are different, but they say the same thing. Indeed, Ockham insists, if a term is connotative, then all of its nominal definitions are synonymous with each other and with the connotative term itself. So there is nothing really deep here, but just a record of how the word 'white' signifies. What's the lesson? **Where connotative terms**

---

[1] In Latin this fact is absolutely clear and obvious, because the nominal definition forces you to put some words in a case other than the nominative case, or to put some of them with a participle:

		album = $_{NDF}$	aliquid	formatum	albedine
Literally:	white = $_{NDF}$	something	formed	by means of a whiteness
		NOMINATIVE	PARTICIPLE	ABLATIVE

The words here are not on equal footing at all. Contrast with this real definition:

	angelus = $_{RDF}$	substantia	intellectualis	et	incorruptiblis
Literally:	angel = $_{RDF}$	a substance	intellectual	[and] incorruptible
	NOMINATIVE	NOMINATIVE		NOMINATIVE

All are on equal footing.

and nominal definitions are at stake, no metaphysics is at stake, and there can be no profound ontological disputes. This claim is also a very important part of Ockham's philosophy, and we will return to it often in the next three chapters.

Ready to Clean House in Metaphysics

During 1302–1317, Ockham passed into adulthood in this intense intellectual environment, which included rigorous training in logic. After finishing the Franciscan version of arts curriculum in London, around 1310 or so (aged around twenty-one), he would have moved on to theology, either in Oxford itself, or in the London *studium*, which was only slightly less prestigious a place to *begin* one's theology training in England. We cannot say, even generally, what classes Ockham took, since there was no set theology curriculum (no fixed set of courses to attend); however, English institutions of higher education did dictate sets of ideas one must learn (from readings or from lectures), and sets of tasks one must competently perform (giving lectures and taking exams). In his own theology training Ockham would have attended lectures on the Bible and on Peter Lombard's *Sentences*, learning thereby how to give such lectures himself. He perhaps even began to draft the outlines of his own commentary on the *Sentences* during the years 1315–1316; the textbook on logic he authored for his own students, which we have been drawing on here, *Summa logicae*, did not come until eight or nine years later.

At the end of this period, in 1317 we find him living as an advanced theology student in the village of Oxford, ready to deliver those *Sentences* lectures, finally able to give his own views on theology and philosophy, within academic convention, and to say how things seemed to him.

Based on what he actually said, we can gather this much about his attitude. Although there were recent Doctors of Theology whose mark on Oxford affected him deeply and positively (such as John Duns Scotus), and though no doubt he also found living teachers there whom he respected, some of what passed for metaphysics at England's own Mecca of learning made him wince. For this reason, armed with the distinctions explained above, Ockham undertook his first great philosophical task—the application of strict logic and sober semantics to clean house in metaphysics.

4

The Teacher at Oxford (1302–1317)

OCKHAM'S CONNOTATION THEORY

As Ockham began the teaching portion of his theology career in 1317, he already showed his determination to correct what he regarded as excesses resulting from the application of Aristotle's theory of the categories. The earliest datable work we have from Ockham is his four-part *Sentences* commentary, begun in 1317.

At this time, *Sentence* commentaries were typically in four parts because the text being commented upon, Peter Lombard's *Sentences*, was also divided into four parts, called 'books'. It was common for an advanced student to distribute his lectures over a two-year academic cycle; he would begin his commentary lectures with Book I of the *Sentences* in the fall semester, moving on to Book II in the spring. The next year he would do Book III in the fall and finish in the spring with Book IV. Ockham seems to have followed exactly this approach in his own *Sentences* commentary, beginning in fall of 1317 and finishing in spring of 1319.

The general process of how *Sentences* lectures came to be published is quite interesting. When an advanced theology student gave commentary lectures on the *Sentences* it was customary to appoint one of the students listening to serve as a more or less official recorder of the lecture, almost like a court reporter today. This person's record of the lectures, called a *reportatio*, could then be given to professional copyists, who would in turn make copies of the lecture on demand for anyone who needed them in their studies. Through a *reportatio*, a philosopher's ideas could get into circulation very quickly, but in a rather unpolished form. If a philosopher's views came under attack or were misrepresented, or if he wanted to build on his *reportatio*, he might undertake a careful reworking of it, changing the wording of one passage, omitting or adding another, and in general cleaning the thing up. Such a polished version of a *Sentences* lecture is sometimes called an *ordinatio* or a *scriptum*, indicating in the first instance that the text has been set in order (Latin *ordo*) by the author himself, or in the second that it has been written (Latin *scriptum*) by the author himself, not by a reporter. Whatever we call these polished texts, the idea is the same: we get something akin to a second edition of a modern book, sometimes with major revisions.

Today we possess *reportatio* versions of Ockham's commentary lectures on Books II-IV of the *Sentences*. But for Book I of his *Sentences* commentary, delivered in the fall of 1317, we no longer have the *reportatio*, instead we have only the *ordinatio*. One reason for this, I think, is that Ockham came out of the gate at the gun, wasting no time in using his logic training to attack contemporary metaphysics. He must have been controversial right from the start, taking up the standard topics for a Book I lecture with gusto—among them whether or not and in what ways theology is a science. Provoking a strong response, it seems Ockham had to clarify some of his ideas, in certain cases adding long provisos to stronger claims he had evidently made in his original lecture.

He had many targets in these early works, but much of his energy was directed against a group of philosophical views we today call *realism*. We will see in detail shortly what certain medieval realists claimed, but briefly we can say that the realists were people who theorized about certain abstract entities, for example, universal essences corresponding to species-terms in language, as we saw in Chapter 2. Ockham's own point of view, called *nominalism*, tended to reject such connections, and to deny the existence of such entities, sometimes by rejecting the possibility their existence outright, sometimes by cleverly attacking the realist's arguments with his theory of terms as we saw it in Chapter 3. It is a testament to his confidence that he attacked the realists so boldly in his earliest lectures at Oxford, and a testament to the controversy generated that we today have only the *ordinatio* of those same lecture, that is, only his revised edition of those lectures.

In the second half of this chapter we will see exactly how Ockham began to use the theory of terms to clean house in metaphysics. But first we need a view of the house itself. What were some of the robust realist theories that Ockham so strongly opposed? What were the arguments and intuitions sustaining them? Once we look at medieval realism constructively and positively, we can begin to examine Ockham's rejection of it. I will do this, not by expositing for you any particular realist or Ockhamist texts, rather, after some basic exposition I will talk through a mock debate between a realist and an Ockhamist. This mock debate will lead us ultimately to a picture of what I call *Ockham's grand nominalism*, his sweeping plan to eliminate a huge part of contemporary, Aristotelian-inspired theorizing as needless, unwarranted, and confused.

Realists

THE PORPHYRIAN TREE

Ultimately, our mediaeval realists derive their theories from Aristotle. If, like good Aristotelians, we think of the world as composed of individual substances with fixed essences, and if we allow our imaginations certain license on the doctrine of the ten categories of being (see in Chapter 2), then, since that doctrine clearly talks about both beings and words, we might begin to imagine what it would be like to understand all of reality as fully and completely *categorized*. Ancient and medieval people were fond of visualizing the result of a complete categorization as a kind of upside-down tree structure, with every existing thing listed under its own proper metaphysical categories, like this:

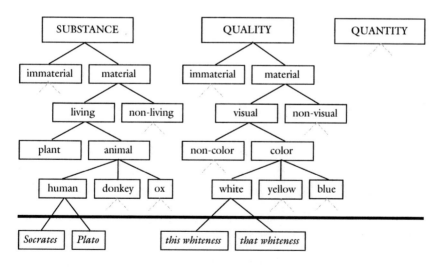

FIGURE 4.1. A Basic Porphyrian Tree

And so on, for each of Aristotle's other seven categories, for a total of ten: SUBSTANCE, QUALITY, QUANTITY, RELATION, TIME, PLACE, POSITION, HAVING, ACTION, and PAS-SION. Such a structure is called a *porphyrian tree*, after the neo-Platonist philosopher Porphyry (d. around 300 c.e.). The thick line near the bottom of the porphyrian tree pictured above is meant to separate the complex system of categories (which lie above the line) from the individuals lying below, which the categories serve to organize. The basis of this system is, obviously, the essences of the individuals thus organized. So the individual Socrates, for example, is essentially human, and so essentially an animal, and so essentially living, and so on, until we reach the category of substance. Similarly, this instance of the color white (*this whiteness* in the chart), is essentially white, and essentially a color, and so on.

The drawing above remains incomplete, of course; the branch-ing dotted lines represent divisions that our example leaves out. Moreover, actual examples of porphyrian trees in medieval manu-scripts often favor the category of substance, and ignore the task of filling out the tree for the other nine categories, just as in the above I have only filled out some branches under substance and quality, and those two only very incompletely. Indeed, how the tree might go in detail for the other categories is anybody's guess. The point is that one can imagine the whole of reality thus categorized according to Aristotle's famous doctrine of the ten categories.

Interpreting the Tree

I will use the idea of a porphyrian tree as a tool for explaining Ockham's critique of metaphysics. To do so I need a picture that represents, albeit only schematically, a fully worked out porphyrian tree. The following picture should be suitable:

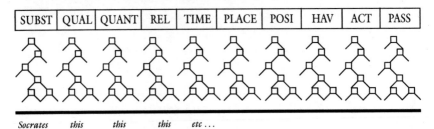

| SUBST | QUAL | QUANT | REL | TIME | PLACE | POSI | HAV | ACT | PASS |

Socrates   *this*   *this*   *this*   *etc ...*
              weakness *2 meters* *similarity*

FIGURE 4.2. Schema of a Complete Porphyrian Tree

We have Aristotle's ten categories at the top, then the genera and species that branch out below each of them, and finally, on the bottom below the thick line, the individuals that fall under these categories. This picture can help us to compare and contrast various philosophical attitudes toward Aristotle's doctrine of the ten categories, and toward the existence of universal essences.

Ultimately we want to use this diagram to understand Ockham and his realist opponents, but it might be useful to begin instead with the simplest possible way of understanding a porphyrian tree, what I will call the *naive interpretation*. On this view, the items below the thick line a porphyrian tree represent *things in the world*, while the items above the line refer, not to pieces of external reality, but rather simply to *category words in our language* that apply truly to the individuals below them in the tree.

On this interpretation, captured in Figure 4.3, language organizes reality, and the chart gives a partial explanation of why certain propositions are true. For example, 'Socrates is an animal' is true because if we trace out the descent relations formed by the branches of the tree (see Figure 4.1), we find that the term 'animal' is above the flesh and blood person *Socrates*, who is at the bottom of the tree. (Here we mean, not that 'animal' is *merely* above Socrates, that is merely higher up, but that it is *linearly* above Socrates in the tree, such that Socrates falls under the node for 'animal'.)

But this view begs an important philosophical question: *Why* does Socrates belong to this category? The proposition 'Socrates is an animal' is true because the chart says it is, but *why* does the

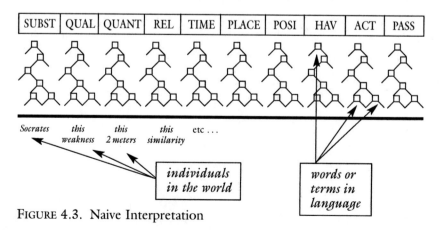

FIGURE 4.3. Naive Interpretation

chart say this? The answer must have something to do with the way Socrates actually is in fact, not merely with how we happen to refer to him. In short, we are interested, not only in what words apply to Socrates ('animal', for instance), but why certain terms with certain meanings correctly apply to Socrates, that is, we want to know *why Socrates is an animal.* Given the Aristotelian assumption that knowledge is objective in some strong sense, we cannot simply say that we apply the word 'animal' to Socrates arbitrarily, assigning categories to things as we like; no. Socrates is an animal, and so is Oscar the ox, and so on. There are objective facts about these objects which the categories in a porphyrian tree reveal and reflect. Thus the naive tree suggests *that* we correctly categorize beings under certain category words, but not *why* we do so. We still need to show why some categorizations are true, others false.

One very basic intuition for why this is so we will call the *realist intuition.* It can be explained by an example as follows. Start with the category SUBSTANCE, and consider the proposition 'Socrates is an animal'. Now, we know this is true, but why is it true? Simple realist answer: because it is in reality as the proposition says it is. Using the apparatus of term logic, we could say that the two categorematic terms in the proposition, 'Socrates' and 'animal', signify a certain relationship between the pieces of reality they pick out. 'Socrates' picks out a thing in the world, and 'animal' picks out something in the world, and the proposition claims they are related in some important metaphysical way. We know what 'Socrates' picks out: a certain individual substance. But what about 'animal'? Well, Aristotle talked about universal essences, did he not? What else would 'animal' refer to but the universal essence <u>animal</u>? Now, the proposition claims that the individual substance Socrates is an animal, which could only mean, given our assumptions so far, that Socrates has the universal essence <u>animal</u> in him somehow. In short we see that because:

   has <u>animal</u> in him.   [Beings]
(Socrates)

the proposition

     'Socrates is an animal'   [Language]

is true. Truth consists in a correspondence between language and
reality:

In fact, this situation explains not only why the proposition
'Socrates is an animal' is a true predication, but why it is a true *essential* predication; that is, not a trivial, accidental fact about Socrates,
but an essential, fundamental one. Similar things could be said for
other true propositions whose terms would be nodes in a porphyrian tree of Aristotle's categories: the terms of each node must somehow refer to a piece of reality; furthermore, if the referents of the
terms in the proposition have the relation the proposition says they
do, then the proposition is true, otherwise not. 'This whiteness is a
color' is true because this whiteness (imagine pointing to the white
part of this page in the book) has the universal essence <u>color</u> in it.
Notice, the key assumption in this realist intuition is that *every significant categorematic term in a true proposition must pick out a true
being in the world.* And in particular, true propositions in which the
predicate is supposed to apply *essentially* to the subject could only
be true because the universal *essence* referred to by the predicate is
in the thing referred to by the subject.

This central aspect of the realist assumption can be captured
graphically using porphyrian trees, but we will need to go beyond
the naive interpretation to do it. The naive interpretation gives us
one tree based on Aristotle's ten categories, with beings on the
bottom and universal essence terms above, but in order to capture
the realist correspondence we have discovered for 'Socrates is an
animal' and similar essential predications, we need to change our
view of the porphyrian tree of categories. Accordingly, the realist
intuition leads us to a *realist interpretation* of the categories, in
which we must imagine, not *one* tree which has beings on the bottom, language on top, but rather *two* distinct porphyrian trees, one
entirely a tree of beings and the other entirely a tree of language.

To begin, picture a *tree of beings*, in which all the items in the
tree are entities in the world. This is easy to swallow if we think
about the individuals in the world, below the thick line in Figure

4.3, but the realist interpretation says more: not only are the individual substances and individual accidents on the bottom level of the tree real, but moreover the categorematic terms in all the boxes above them signify real beings. In particular, the realities signified by the terms in those boxes are *universal essences,* or more simply, *universals.* The universal essences lower down in the branches of the tree, but still above the thick line, are *species,* while those higher up are *genera.* A universal, remember, is supposed to be a piece of external reality, for example, <u>animal</u>, which is somehow shared as a whole, all at once, as an ingredient of all the individuals that are in fact animals. Putting all this together, the first step of our realist interpretation would yield a tree of beings such as this:

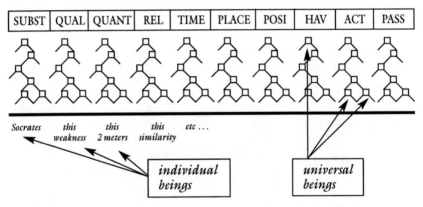

FIGURE 4.4. Realist Tree of Beings

Perhaps no human could ever actually comprehend such a tree, since doing so would constitute a perfect and complete scientific map of reality, organizing an enormous collection of universal essences, <u>human</u>, <u>donkey</u>, <u>animal</u>, <u>material</u>, <u>color</u>, and so on, in addition to the billions of individual substances at the bottom. Still, Aristotle's doctrine of the categories does imply that such a thing could be objectively comprehended. Maybe God could do it.

Moreover, for the realist interpretation we must also admit a *tree of language,* in which the scientifically correct relationships between our categorematic terms are represented. In such a tree all the nodes will be terms in some language (for ease we can imagine it is the mental language all human beings share):

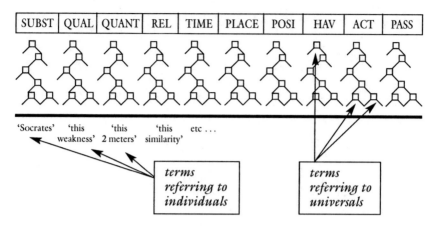

FIGURE 4.5. REALIST TREE OF LANGUAGE

Notice the quotation marks around each item; this is a tree of names, not of things. Now, a tree like this would be like a correct map of scientific terminology. Again, no one has ever or could ever actually make such a language map at this tree represents—what book is large enough to hold it?—still, it must be in principle possible that such a map could exist.

Having imagined these two trees, one of beings and one of terms, the heart of the realist view is now easy to state: there is a simple mapping between these two trees, because there is an immediate connection between language and the world: *the world* (that is, *non-linguistic reality*) has a porphyrian tree structure, and correctly organized scientific *language* also has this very same tree structure. Quite simply, according to the realist interpretation, the order of language maps one-to-one directly onto the order of being, node for node. In short, the fact that we have true propositions with essential predications shows that we have the sort of correspondences we saw above:

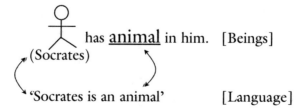

only for every single node of each tree:

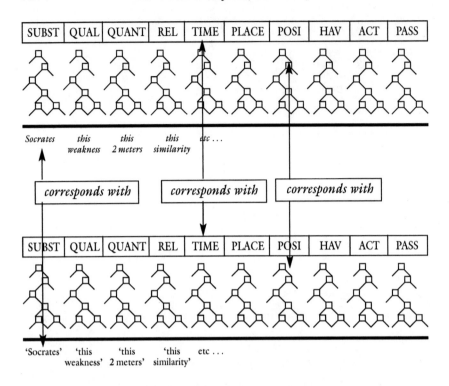

FIGURE 4.6. How the Realist Sees the World-Language Connection

For example, corresponding to the universal categorematic term 'human', there must exist in reality a universal essence, humanity, and corresponding to the universal categorematic term 'brown' there must be a universal essence brown, and so on.

Truth is explained using these trees exactly as we explained it above. Consider 'Socrates is an animal'. If we look at a tree of beings, we see the universal essence animal is in a branch above the individual Socrates, which means that this essence animal is a part of the element of reality we call Socrates; and precisely what the proposition says is that this is so. The proposition reflects reality; therefore it is true. *This* piece of language (the proposition 'Socrates is an animal') is true because these pieces of reality (Socrates and the universal essence animality) are like *that*. 'Socrates is a plant' is false for similar reasons; Socrates does not actually contain the universal plant in him. The tree of beings shows this deep truth, because in it Socrates does not fall under the category plant; *therefore* the proposition saying he does is false.

Similar remarks apply to all ten categories: the truth of 'This whiteness is a color', for example. This new interpretation of the porphyrian tree will provide what the naive interpretation seemed to lack; that is, the new view provides a richer picture of why some propositions are true and some false, how propositions get to be true and false, and more importantly, why some predications are essential.

However, we should also notice that, compared with the naive interpretation, on the realist interpretation we have to believe in the existence of lots more entities. Philosophers use the word *ontology* to mean the set of entities that a particular person believes are real, or that a particular theory supposes to be real. The point here is that the realist interpretation has a much larger ontology than the naive interpretation. In the naive interpretation, there were individual substances below the line and category words above. This is entirely unobjectionable. Everyone has as part of her ontology both individual substances (like Socrates and Maggie Magnolia and this whiteness, and so forth) and also category words (like 'human' and 'plant' and 'color'). No problem there; people are real and the word 'people' is real. But the realist interpretation seems to expand ontology to an incredible degree; for each node in the tree of language—that is, corresponding to each significant categorematic term that can be essentially predicated in a proposition—we must admit the existence of a *corresponding node* in the tree of beings. Because 'Socrates is an animal' is a true essential predication, the realist says, we must admit into our ontology both the individual person Socrates and the universal <u>animal</u>. In order to explain truth we seem constrained to accept as real, and so to admit into our ontology, many universal essences. This proliferation might make you uncomfortable.

The Realist Interpretation Extended

If you are uncomfortable now, just wait. Once we start thinking in a realist vein like this there is really no reason to stop short. The realist intuition that there is a fairly direct one-to-one correspondence between the significant terms in our language and beings in reality can be extended to many situations beyond those we have so far considered. For example, we can form perfectly intelligible propositions using terms 'higher up' in the language tree, such as these: 'Every animal is living,' 'Every color is a quality,' or 'Every human being is a substance'. These propositions, which we might regard as truths of Aristotelian-style metaphysics, are not about concrete individuals, according to the realist, but are nevertheless about certain entities in the world; they are about the relationship between certain relatively lower-level universals essences to other, higher-level ones. For example, 'Every animal is living' is true because on the tree of beings <u>animal</u> is grouped under <u>living things</u>, and this is reflected in the tree of language, and in the proposition itself. By applying this understanding to all the statements of Aristotelian metaphysics, the objectivity of knowledge, so important to Aristotle's conception of science, is evidently assured; genus and species terms are not classifications that we impose on reality, but are pieces of language that have signification—and in propositions like those above, they also have supposition and truth-value—because of how they reflect unseen universal realities. Genus and species are real, their relations objective, and therefore metaphysics is a science.

Riding even further downstream on the realist current, we can make similar arguments without referring to the prophyrian tree structure at all. For example, take a concrete term like 'human being' and make from it an abstract noun, 'humanity'. Then use the abstract noun as a grammatical subject in a proposition to get a perfectly reasonable statement according to Aristotelian philosophy, for example 'Humanity is an essence'. This is a true proposition in Aristotelian philosophy because it is in reality as the proposition says; humanity *is* an essence, in fact, it is the essence of any human being. So, it might seem, many truths of Aristotelian science can be phrased this way. But this obviously suggests that, corresponding to the significant utterance 'animality', there must be some thing, <u>animality</u>, which corresponds to the term in the true proposition.

In general, the realist holds that science is about a structured reality of real individuals and the universals that shape them. Which individuals and universals? Language tells you. How many are there? Again, language tells you. For 'Humanity is an essence' to be true, the thing the subject term stands for must contain the thing the predicate stands for. So reality must have in it a thing, <u>humanity</u>, and certain things, <u>essences</u>, if 'Humanity is an essence' is true, the one must stand to the others as the proposition says it does.

Similarly, if physics is the science of motion, there must be something for physics to be about, and so there must be a thing in the world, <u>motion</u>, corresponding to the categorematic term 'motion'. What is <u>motion</u>? Realists in Ockham's time tended to view it as an accidental form which inheres in an individual substance while it is moving, and which is the cause of that thing's motion. It is the inherence (or lack thereof) of this accidental form <u>motion</u> in a substance X that makes propositions of the form 'X is moving' true (or false).

To take a final example we will have occasion to discuss later, suppose page 20 and page 91 of this book are similar, in that they are both white. (They each have black print added to them, of course, and different print at that, but both pages are able to receive and to show their black print because their basic coloring is white.) Since they are both white, 'Page 20 and page 91 are similar' is true. Now in the tree of language 'similar' is a kind of relation—that is, it falls under the category of RELATION—and so for the realist, there must be some accidental form in reality, <u>similarity</u>, which falls in reality under the accidental category RELATION in the tree of beings. The picture we get is that 'Page 20 and page 91 are similar' is true because page 20 has an accident, <u>white</u>, and page 91 has an accident, <u>white</u>, *and* each page has an occurrence of *another accidental form*, viz., <u>similarity</u>, one form in page 20, based in its whiteness, and one in page 91, based on its whiteness. On this story, six different entities are needed to make 'Page 20 and page 91 are similar' true. The proposition requires that page 20 and page 91 be real (2), that each of their whitenesses must be real (+2), and their similarities must be real too (+2). We might not have imagined that things like <u>similarities</u> exist in the world, but since $2 + 2 + 2 = 6$, we see how language has shown us the surprisingly fecund invisible structure of reality. How else could this (or any other) proposition be true, unless reality exactly mirrored language?

Hopefully, through these examples the realist strategy is beginning to emerge: from what we know about language, we reason back to the nature of reality; we can read the structure of reality off of the structure of language. In this way, the realist likes to reason *from* language *to* hidden metaphysical realities.

The Basic Ockhamist Approach

In fairness, it is possible that no one person in the Middle Ages made all of the arguments and believed in all of the entities that I describe above; there may have been no one person who was a realist in the full sense specified here. But all of the strategies and arguments I mention can be found in the work of important thinkers of Ockham's day, people such as Walter Chatton and Walter Burley. Ockham opposed these arguments as they occurred in the writings of others, but even more, in his own positive philosophizing Ockham stated his general opposition to the whole spirit of this approach to metaphysics. Before we look at the details of his attack on particular realist arguments and entities, it will be instructive to build a realist case for a modern example, and then see how Ockham would respond to this hypothetical case. My hope is to focus the reader's mind on the intuitive heart of Ockham's general aversion to realism before examining the detailed methods of his counter-case.

In an interview in 2004, for an article discussing how illiteracy in America affects health care, eminent American physician Dr. John D. Nelson observed that a lack of general health knowledge is an impediment to proper self-care for many patients. Both written and spoken medical instructions are often misunderstood. Nelson noted that the problem of misunderstanding is exacerbated by the strong feelings associated with a frightening diagnosis, which render people even more susceptible to misunderstand important medical information. The interview reads:

> There can also be an emotional component. "It's a different kind of understanding," Nelson said. "The emotionality that occurs when any medical process or procedure goes on is intense. You hear some of the words. You don't hear all of the words."

Even though we understand Nelson's point clearly, the second sentence of this quotation contains the unusual word "emotionality". What on earth is *emotionality*? If we take the realist attitude we have been exploring, we are forced to say that, if what Nelson says is true (as it seems to be), then this is because there is a thing in the world, emotionality, corresponding to the term 'emotionality', and it must be the case that this thing, emotionality, sometimes stalks us when we learn about needing a risky medical procedure. But this seems frankly bizarre. What Nelson means is not that some entity, emotionality, overcomes us as we listen to a doctor describe a process of risk and potential suffering, but rather that certain *emotions* overcome us—just ordinary emotions, such as *fear, anticipation*, or *anger*. The realist turn would lead to a very strange result if we followed it in this case; in addition to such feelings as fear, anticipation, or anger, we would have to posit another entity, <u>emotionality</u>, which is—what? A blend of all the above? The Platonic Form of emotion? Clearly, here is a case where the realist impulse would lead too far, and so would lead us astray if we followed it. Indeed, rather than say 'The emotionality . . . is intense', it might be better to say 'The emotions . . . are intense'. There is no temptation to hypostasize this and see a new entity <u>emotionality</u> once we recognize that only language is involved here, since emotions are already real, normal elements of reality, and they are individual, concrete events in the world, not universals at all.

But even if it is transparently strange in this context, the general pull of the realist picture is strong. We can imagine that if that the word 'emotionality' came into wide and unreflective use in English, in two hundred years we might see people giving theories of <u>emotionality</u> as a separate entity; we might have university departments of emotionality studies; philosophers would find they had to ask 'What is the metaphysical status of emotionality'? But does this give us a reason to say there is such a thing as emotionality? And if not, then what is emotionality?

Were he alive to see such a thing, Ockham would answer this way: "It's just a word someone made up. Someone went from 'emotions' → 'emotionality', made a sentence, and two hundred years later everybody thought it involved *metaphysics*."

What led us astray? The realist assumption that language maps onto the real world *simply*. Ockham put the general point this way in the *ordinatio* of Book I of his *Sentences* commentary lecture, first delivered around 1317:

> Whence it is, I believe, that many are deceived . . . they have it that there are as many distinct things as there are significant utterances, so that there is as great a distinction among things signified as there is among significant utterances. (Book I, Distinction 1; unless otherwise noted, all translations are my own)

In other words, the damaging assumption is the one pictured in Figure 4.6 above, that the structure of language and the structure of reality map onto each other simply, one-to-one, node for node.

Now, if you want to understand Ockham's critique of meta-physics, take my 'emotionality' example and apply it to 'animals' → 'animality', 'humans' → 'humanity' or even to 'moving things' → 'motion'. This is the gist of Ockham's attack on realist meta-physics.

Remember Your Logic . . .

Ockham executes this attack with a virtuoso application of the prin-ciples of logic that we discussed in the last chapter. To illustrate how this works I have constructed a mock debate between Ockham and a realist that shows precisely how Ockham tended to apply the the-ory of terms to dismantling the realist interpretation. The reader will recognize that each of the lessons we learned about the nature of terms in Chapter 3 occurs here again in boldface type.

The realist begins our conversation:

REALIST: My claim is simply that, if a term makes a difference to the truth of a proposition in which it occurs, it must sig-nify, or at least supposit for, a real thing. How else are truth and reference supposed to work if not this way or something close to it?

OCKHAM: What about syncategorematic terms, for example 'all' or 'only'? **Some terms are logically significant, in other words significant to truth, without really meaning anything on their own.** So you are mistaken at the outset; it is not generally true that a term must pick out an element of reality in order to be usefully employed in saying true things about the world.

REALIST: No problem. I will limit myself to categorematic terms only. In fact, we can even consider only the categore-matic terms under the category of substance in the por-phyrian tree. Surely *these* terms obey the principle I articulated above. For 'Animal is a substance' and 'Socrates is an animal' to be true, there must be animality, to which the term 'animal' refers, and so on.

OCKHAM: And animality signifies . . . what? The universal essence <u>animal</u>? Universal essences cannot possibly exist (see below), and besides, all you have really done here is to ignore the distinction between first/second intention terms, and also first/second imposition terms. **We must be very careful to distinguish situations in which we are talking about language, versus situations when we are talking about non-language, and similarly to distinguish when we are talking about mental things versus non-mental things; in particular, we must be careful to distinguish cases where we are really talking about concepts in subtle ways, that is, cases where we are using terms of first imposition and second intention.** The word 'animal' is certainly categorematic, and it sometimes is absolute, and then it refers to a real thing, not to language; it is then first imposition, like 'deer' when pointing to a deer. But 'animal' is not first imposition in the proposition 'Animal is a genus', for we do not intend (pointing to a deer, say) that this flesh and blood mammal is a genus! That would be obviously false. Categorematically, 'animal' does not supposit here for a thing in the world like a deer, but rather only for the spoken or written terms $animal_s$ or $animal_w$, which terms themselves apply to actual deer and saber-toothed tigers, and so forth. Possibly in 'Animal is a genus', 'animal' names a term, and the proposition simply means this: the term 'animal' is a genus-term. In such a situation the term 'animal' would have material supposition, not personal supposition; it would refer to a piece of language only. More likely in 'Animal is a genus' we are thinking of where the concept $animal_m$ falls in conceptual space, in which case 'Animal is a genus' means that 'animal' is a genus-concept, and 'animal' has simple supposition. But certainly not personal supposition; in this case it does not refer to the external, nonlinguistic world.

REALIST: Perhaps this response will work with terms under substance in the porphyrian tree, but I have extended my analysis to more useful and subtle cases, for example, 'motion'. Physics is a real science, the science of motion. So we think this is true: 'Physics is the science of motion'. Hence motion is a real thing in the world; who would deny this? The entity <u>motion</u> is that thing which the term 'motion' picks out, and it is this entity, <u>motion</u>, that makes 'Physics is the science of motion' true. Would you say that motion isn't real?

OCKHAM: 'Motion' is indeed a categorematic term, and categorematic terms make a difference to truth; they supposit
in various ways in the propositions in which they occur. But
they do not always do so in a simple, referential way,
although what you now presume is that every categorematic term is metaphysically significant. Which is to say:
you have wrongly assumed that every categorematic term
we have discussed is an absolute term, since **where
absolute terms and real definitions are at stake, metaphysics is at stake, and there can be profound ontological disputes about the entities thus signified.** But what
if I could show that, in fact, some terms, such as 'motion',
'time', and 'similar', were connotative instead? What would
happen if they were? **Where connotative terms and nominal definitions are at stake, no metaphysics is at stake,
and there can be no profound ontological disputes.**
Hence if 'motion' were just a connotative name, a mere
definition or abbreviation, then your assumption of simple,
direct correspondence goes by the board, and we could
show that we need not posit an entity <u>motion</u> even though
'Physics is about motion' is a perfectly significant, and
indeed, is even a true proposition.

Ockham's Grand Nominalism

What happens to our Aristotelian metaphysics if we follow
Ockham and take this mode of reply? How much do we have to
give up if we drop the two realist assumptions that: (1) we can easily read the structure of reality off of the structure of language, and
(2) every categorematic term in the porphyrian tree is an absolute
term, and so is metaphysically significant?

Quite a bit, as it happens. To see how much, and so to catch a
glimpse of the general scope of Ockham's own positive metaphysical views (before we go on to examine some details in the two
chapters that follow), we start afresh with the porphyrian tree and
the ten categories. Let us recall the diagram that started off the
realist line of argument in Figure 4.2 on the next page.

Ockham's taming of the wild proliferation of entities that
seemed to follow as we move from the naive interpretation to the
realist interpretation can be grouped into three stages, all of which

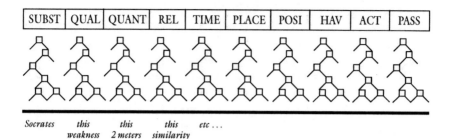

| SUBST | QUAL | QUANT | REL | TIME | PLACE | POSI | HAV | ACT | PASS |

Socrates   *this*   *this*   *this*   *etc . . .*
        weakness *2 meters* *similarity*

FIGURE 4.2. Schema of a Complete Porphyrian Tree

refer to these trees: (1) he clarified generally the relationship between language and reality; (2) he radically pruned the branching structures in the middle of the picture; and (3) he lopped off almost the whole of the right-hand side of the tree. Although Ockham himself did not argue all this through as a three-stage process, it is very convenient to explain the process by such a device, and so we will sketch the three stages just listed in that order.

Stage I. The Tree of Language

Ockham would not really object to thinking of two distinct trees, one tree of language and one of beings. But he would reject the idea that the tree of language contains terms that must connect with entities in the world node for node, and that the two trees must mirror each other exactly for us to explain truth.

We can use the theory of terms to reject this aspect of the realist picture. Start by focusing just on the realist's tree of language. In the first stage of an Ockham-style critique we can ask: What if the terms in the boxes above the thick line in the tree of language are *second impositions?* For example, as noted above, if we understand the term 'animal' in 'Animal is a genus' to be a term of second imposition, then 'Animal is a genus' means no more or no less than '"Animal" is a genus-term'. Hence it does not require for its truth that the term 'animal' signify some real being, a universal essence <u>animal</u>, which is also a species, but only that the term 'animal' is in fact a genus-term, which it indeed is. All we are saying is that 'animal' occurs above the line as a node in a porphyrian tree of language, but not at the bottom level of such nodes (the species-level). 'Animal' is a category word, but not the lowest level of category word. Or again, Ockham could say that the way to understand a true proposition such as 'Socrates is an animal' is that the term 'animal' supposits personally for something for which the term 'Socrates' also personally supposits, namely, Socrates.

Notice, without assuming that 'animal' names anything in the world, Ockham's theory of terms shows not only why 'animal' is in a branch above 'Socrates' in a correct tree of language, but also how the proposition 'Socrates is an animal' gets to be true. This is something the naive interpretation could not do, and which the realist did only by insisting on a one-to-one connection between the tree of language and the tree of beings. Consequently, if we could extend these kinds of analyses to other nodes in the tree of language we would lose a significant reason for thinking that the terms above the line in the tree of language had to correspond to similar nodes in a tree of beings at all. So should we totally abandon the idea of a tree of language?

No need for that; it is possible to record the linguistic facts that (1) 'animal' is a genus, and that (2) 'animal' is above 'Socrates' in a proper tree of language, and so is truly predicated of it, using something like a porphyrian tree. Ockham could accept that there is a tree of language, just as the realist believed, but he would give his own interpretation to the terms above the thick line in any tree of language:

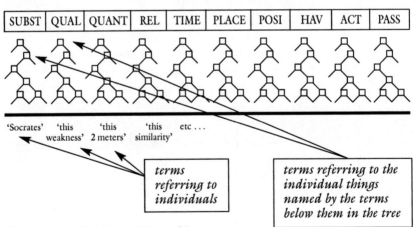

FIGURE 4.7. Ockham's Tree of Language

The point is that to do so does not to imply any simple isomorphism with the structure of the world, since we no longer need the realist assumption of corresponding nodes to explain truth.

Ockham does not therefore believe that we make up the concept animal_m out of nowhere, and that there aren't really animals. There are animals, and the similarities between animals are real, but they are not some one *thing* in the way the realist imagines they must be, and certainly the existence of one *term* in regard to a phenomenon does not by itself license the positing of exactly one *thing* corresponding to it. The grouping of animal similarities no more implies the existence of a unified entity <u>animality</u> answering to the grouping term 'animal' any more than 'the set of all foods I ate yesterday' implies the existence of a unified entity <u>yesterday-ate-foodity</u>. Yet for all that, this can still be a true general proposition: 'The set of all foods I ate yesterday includes ice cream'.

"But," the realist might reply, "how then will we explain *why* the term 'animal' so signifies in a proposition such as 'Socrates is an animal'? You say how 'Socrates is an animal' is true but not why it is true. To explain this relational fact between language and the non-linguistic world—in particular the fact that 'animal' has personal supposition in this proposition—the term 'animal' must invoke some non-linguistic entity, some animal ingredient in Socrates, surely. As 'animal' is a universal term, it must therefore invoke a universal ingredient."

Stage II. Rejection of Universal Essences

To see Ockham's response to this legitimate question, let us set aside the tree of language completely and focus instead on the realist tree of being. According to Ockham's approach, not only does the tree of language give us no good reason to posit an exactly corresponding tree of beings, but even further, it is impossible that there exist a tree of beings at all if you insist that the nodes above the line must be universal essences. In effect, Ockham would prune the realist tree of beings vertically, rejecting even the *possibility* of having universal essences in the middle of the tree.

He does this by arguing at length that universals essences are simply impossible entities; there is no consistent theory explaining the manner of their existence. Some of his arguments are very difficult and technical. Fortunately, there are two which are quite accessible and yet still quite powerful. To understand his arguments against universals it is important to remind ourselves briefly what a universal essence is supposed to be.

The realists to whom Ockham was reacting in his *Sentences* commentary thought of a universal essence of an individual substance *a* of type *T* as the what-it-is-to-be *T*, and as realists they insisted that the what-it-is-to-be *T* of *a* is just as real as *a* itself, and was distinct from *a* as well. For example, Maggie Magnolia is a tree, and so is of the type 'tree', and so there must exist in her a certain entity, the what-it-is-to-be-a-tree, i.e., or as we have been saying here, the essence <u>tree</u>. This <u>tree</u> is just as real as Maggie is, and is quite distinct from her; it is not just the sum of her tree-like properties or something like that. Moreover, since there are usually several individuals of any given type, and since each is equally a representative of that type, all individuals *a*, *b* of a type *T* must have the what-it-is-to-be *T* in them at the same time; that is, the what-it-is-to-be *T* is in *a* and in *b* at the same time. For instance, Maggie Magnolia and Margaret Magnolia are both trees, and so are of the type 'tree', and so there must exist in them both, at the same time, a certain entity, the what-it-is-to-be-a-tree, or as we have been representing it, the essence <u>tree</u>. This essence is what makes Maggie and Margaret trees, and it is what explains both their metaphysical similarity to each other (both being trees), and also how we know them both as trees (see Chapter 2). Nor must we imagine that Maggie has but a part of <u>tree</u> while Margaret has another part of <u>tree</u>; these two individuals are both equally trees, and so both must have the essence <u>tree</u> as an ingredient, as a *whole*, at the same time. This is the really odd bit, to most people: according to the realists essences have the odd property of belonging as a whole to completely distinct things at the same time, effectively existing as a whole now here (in Maggie), and as a whole now there too (in Margaret). It is for this reason that essences were called 'universal': they are supposed to be everywhere their individual instances are, as a whole all at once. Very strange beings indeed.

Now Ockham argues that there is absolutely no way a being meeting this description can possibly exist in this or any other world. Universal essences are simply impossible. One of his most famous and effective arguments against the possibility of such things is as follows. If the universal <u>human being</u> and individual human beings (for example) are really distinct, then it is possible for them to exist separately; one can exist while the other does not, and vice versa. But then God, who can do anything that does not involve a contradiction, could destroy utterly all the individual human beings, and still preserve the universal essence <u>human being</u>. In that case there would be a universal essence of certain things, but without the things. Even worse, God could destroy utterly <u>human being</u> and preserve all the individual humans. In that case, there could be existing individuals of essentially the same kind, but with no existing universal essence.

A second Ockhamist argument against universals runs as follows. Many realists argued that at least one ingredient of Socrates's essence is the universal <u>human being</u>, and that this universal is really distinct from Socrates. Now ask: Do Socrates and the universal <u>human being</u> together make up some *one individual thing*? If you say yes, then Socrates is not individual, but only a part of an individual, like form and matter are parts of individuals. If on the other hand you say no, then the composed thing *Socrates/Socrates's essence* has no unity, and so is not a proper, coherent whole (like an assembled plastic model kit) but is rather a heap in which each part is self-sufficient (like a pile of unassembled plastic model parts). Socrates and his essence would not be tightly connected. But this would violate Aristotle's idea that individual substances are proper, coherent wholes, and it would push us back to Plato's view of essences as distinct, independent Forms, which most thinkers in the medieval period agreed was untenable.

Back to the tree of beings. Since Ockham rejected universals, his tree of being would have to cut out as impossible all the nodes above the thick line, that is, above the level of individuals. The net effect is to take Figure 4.4 and strip out the middle, collapsing the tree of beings *vertically*. We can picture the new situation like this:

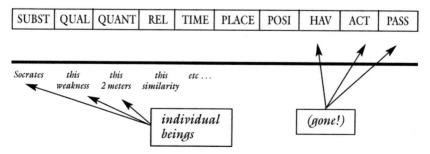

FIGURE 4.8. Ockham's "Tree" of Beings, Intermediate Version

We leave the big category boxes at the top to remind us what we are dealing with, and because there are still individuals below them all the way down at the bottom, but these category boxes do not represent universal essences either, on Ockham's view. There is nothing whatsoever in reality that is, in any metaphysically interesting sense, universal. Ockham admitted that there was a sense in which general categorematic terms, whether spoken or written or mental, are universal, in that they are capable of signifying and *suppositing for* many things at once. But the claim that any element of reality is universal by *existing* in many things at once, this he utterly rejects, leading to the situation pictured above.

Notice, though, there are still some weird entities in Figure 4.8: this two meters (pointing to a two-meter tall person) is an entity, and, presumably, *that* two meters (pointing at another such person), and *that other* two meters over there, are all entities. Moreover, we have this similarity and that similarity, and so on. Something will need to be done about this.

Stage III. Connotation Theory

Reality is already a lot smaller, and the tree of beings really isn't a tree anymore, but only a bunch of individual entities falling under ten categories. More of a stump, really. However, this was still too much for Ockham; in metaphysics a narrow stump is better than a wide one, and since he did not believe in the existence of this, that, and the other similarity, he tried to collapse the categories of being not only *vertically*, but also *horizontally*. To put it more precisely, he tried to show not only that there are no real entities of any kind above the level of individuals, that is, that there are no universals, he also tried to show that there are no real individuals below the line in any categories besides SUBSTANCE and QUALITY. In effect, he argued that we could lop off the right-most eight of the nine accidental categories in the "tree" of beings in Figure 4.8 above. The style of argument for this horizontal collapse is more varied, and will take some explanation.

As we have already seen, the realist effectively assumes that every categorematic term is an absolute term. What if we could show that, in fact, some important terms in metaphysics, such as 'motion', 'time', or 'similar', were connotative instead? To reuse a previous example, the realist, assuming 'similar' is an absolute

term, has a method of explaining why, on the basis of the whiteness in pages 20 and 91 of this book, the proposition 'Page 20
and page 91 are similar' is true. It runs this way: page 20 and
page 91 must be real (2), each of their individual whitenesses
must be real (+2), and each of their similarities must be real too
(+2). Hence 2 + 2 + 2 = 6 entities exist.

But can we explain the situation another way? For example,
suppose that 'similar' were merely a connotative term with the following nominal definition:

similar $=_{NDF}$ something that has such a quality as another
thing has

Remember, connotative terms are synonymous with their nominal
definitions. So they are completely equivalent in meaning, signifying all the same things in all the same ways. So 'similar' signifies no
more and no less than what all the categorematic terms occurring
in its nominal definition signify—in other words, no more and no
less than: 'something that has such a quality as another thing has'.
Since the definition and the word it defines are equivalent, we can
substitute the definition for the term it defines. By performing
such a substitution in the true sentence 'Page 20 and page 91 are
similar', we see that this sentence in fact does not imply the existence of two relative accidents of <u>similarity</u>, which to the realist,
unmindful of the absolute/connotative distinction, thought it did.
For 'Page 20 and page 91 are similar' means no more and no less
than 'Page 20 has such a quality as page 91 has'. (Or, if you want
to be strict about it, 'Page 20 and Page 91 are [each] something[s]
that have such a quality as another thing has'. That is, 20 has a
quality like 91 and vice versa.)

Now, with this analysis in front of us, let's try to reason like a
realist, from language back to the world, and count the entities
using our new, equivalent sentence 'Page 20 has such a quality as
page 91 has'. What are the absolute categorematic terms in this
sentence? 'Page 20,' which refers to the individual substance page
20 in this book, 'page 91,' which refers to the individual substance
page 91, and the term 'quality', which is the name of an accidental category, and in this example indirectly refers to the two whitenesses in the two pages. So, which of the ten categories are
represented by the categorematic terms of this true, equivalent

sentence? Only two: substance and quality. So which categories must we say are real in order to explain the truth of 'Page 20 and page 91 are similar'? *Only two: substance and quality.* There is no real entity such as <u>similarity</u> in the world, and less cause to think that the category RELATION contains real beings at all.

Let us be clear. Two individual substances can be really related by being similar, certainly. Pages 20 and 91 are really white, and so are really similar, and are really so related. However, once we recognize that 'similar' is just a connotative term abbreviating a longer nominal definition which itself refers only to substances and their qualities, it's plain that the only *entities* we can validly infer from this situation are two individual substances, pages 20 and 91 (2 entities), and their individual white qualities, that is, page 20's whiteness and page 91's whiteness (+2 entities). Thus there are 2 + 2 = 4 entities in *two* categories here, not 6 entities in *three*, as the realist had concluded by assuming that 'similar' is an absolute term.

Now, what if we could do this same trick for all the other terms under the category of RELATION, and even for the other categories on the right of quality, that is, those terms in the tree under TIME, PLACE, and so forth? We would give their nominal definitions, and somehow show that the definitions only signify individual substances and individual qualities. Would we not then have shown that there is no need to posit ten categories of *beings*, even if we agree that there are ten categories of *words*? For the most part, Ockham thinks we can get along with just two categories of beings (they are—you will already have guessed it—SUBSTANCE and QUALITY), and he thinks that there is no philosophical reason to posit real individuals in the other eight categories at all. Hence we can cut more or less the entire right-hand side of the diagram off, category boxes and individuals included.

Applying this to Figure 4.8 gives us a picture of Ockham's view of reality, represented in Fig. 4.9 on the next page.

The ghostly figure of the category of RELATION still haunts the diagram because Ockham believed in the reality of some relations, not on account of anything in Aristotelian philosophy or in reason, but only on account of the demands of religion: for example, in the trinity the son must be really related to the father and vice versa, and so there must exist paternity and filiality as real things.

Setting this theological exception aside, what, according to William Ockham, are the things that are real? Well, just look at the

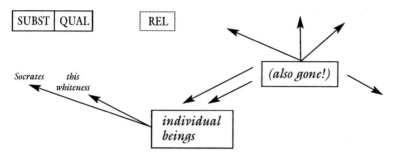

FIGURE 4.9. Ockham's "Tree" of Beings, Final Version

picture. What is real is only this: individual substances and their individual qualities. *That's it.*

Let us be clear about what this means. Time, for example, is not a real part of the world. There is no entity time. Again, with ACTION and PASSION, if A causes B, it is not because A has an active causal accident and B has a passive causal accident. Causality is not a separate real accident existing in the world. One thing really causes another, to be sure. But causality is not a separate thing in the world. Perhaps most shocking, he extends this method, which we could call *connotative reduction,* to show that there is no entity motion. There are individual substances that are moving temporally, to be sure. But they do not move because they take on an accident motion. (We will see this in detail in Chapter 6.)

Obviously, this last stage of his grand nominalism is not a coda to the symphony but is rather the chief movement. Although it is less famous today than his razor, say, this magnificent application of connotation theory is one of Ockham's central claims to fame.

Is Simpler Better?

I hope the reader has a sense of why I call this 'Ockham's *grand* nominalism'. However, strictly speaking, Ockham did not and could not actually carry the entire program out to its conclusion. Since the realist imagines an entity corresponding to *each node* in the full porphyrian tree of beings, it was simply too grand for any one person to carry out a connotative reduction of all of those nodes in the eight categories Ockham would want us to reduce. To complete each reduction fully, we would assume the term in question to be connotative, then present a suitable and plausible nominal definition of it, the new terms of which are all absolute and which only refer to individuals or their individual qualities. To do this for every node of the tree would seem impossible for one person. But there is an even more serious problem. As he carried out his lecture duties in Oxford and in London, Ockham began to work out how to do this connotative reduction for several important cases—for 'similarity', as I have shown above, and later also for 'motion', as I will show in Chapter 6—his results became known to other philosophers, and he began to meet resistance. But then, in trying to support connotation theory against its opponents, he came to see that a crucial piece of the argument was underdeveloped.

The reader may have already begun to descry the gap herself, which is this: just because connotative reduction gives a simpler picture of reality—for example, it explains the truth of 'Page 20 and page 91 are similar' using four entities instead of six—is this any reason for us to follow the simpler account? In short, why prefer a narrow trunk to a broad trunk in metaphysics? Just because we can reduce the categories horizontally doesn't mean we should or that we must. In his grand nominalism, Ockham sometimes claims the realist is confused and flatly mistaken (for example, in supposing that that universals exist, or that every significant utterance signifies a being), but often he merely offers a simpler *alternative account* of how propositions get to be true and false, that is, a simpler *alternative semantics*, the central tool of which is his theory of terms, and in particular connotation theory. But why prefer this simpler account? The realist explains truth, Ockham explains truth; the two only disagree on how many entities are required to do it. But other than the inherent charm and subtlety of connotation theory, is there anything about the relative simplicity of its ontology that recommends it for our acceptance, and which correlatively discredits the realist view?

Well, there is, if you put a premium on simpler explanations and smaller ontologies. In short, there is, if you accept a principle like Ockham's razor: *pluralitas non ponenda est sine necessitate.* A plurality ought not be accepted without necessity. And so, at the close of 1319, to shore up his grand nominalism, Ockham became a champion of the principle, which, although not invented by him, is still associated with his name seven hundred years later. The new teacher had found his niche.

5

The Teacher Attacked
(1319–1321)

RAZORS AND ANTI-RAZORS

From this point on in Ockham's life we find controversy, and the drama includes several specific historical figures whose relationship to Ockham is more clearly understood. If previously we have only been speculating on the identity of his teachers, his colleagues, and who was influencing whom, after 1319 the fire of Ockham's controversial views and actions shed a much clearer light on the personalities involved.

One of the most significant figures to circulate in Ockham's world in this period and the next was Walter Chatton. Chatton was probably younger than Ockham by at least two years, or perhaps by as many as five, and he hailed from the far north of England. His mid-career path was quite similar to Ockham's—he joined the Franciscans as a young man, trained early at provincial Franciscan schools, was singled out by his talents for advancement to theology training in London and Oxford. After 1324, their careers could not have been more different: upon completing his Oxford doctorate, Chatton eventually became an important advisor to the Avignon popes, and was finally appointed a bishop, although he died before assuming office. During this same time Ockham, having been side-tracked on his doctorate, was fleeing for his life from the power at Avignon. The only thing he would earn from the pope was excommunication.

As a philosopher, Chatton was a realist, but he did not accept all the realist arguments and conclusions we examined in the last chapter; he was rather more fussy about his realism. To take an example, he did not believe we had to posit similarity in the category RELATION. However, he believed in the reality of all ten categories of being, and was quite straightforwardly a realist about some other entities in relational categories (for example, in RELA-TION, ACTION, or PASSION). In particular, he believed in the reality of causal relations between actor and receiver, such as between a producer and the thing it produces, and also in certain accidental entities not straightforwardly comprehended by the porphyrian tree, such as a form <u>motion</u> that inheres in a moving substance when something causes it to have local motion. And like most realists, Chatton thought that real, objective science was about real, objective things in the world, and so believed in the literal reality of causality and of motion, within an Aristotelian framework.

It is very clear from the historical record that Chatton opposed Ockham's grand nominalism very vocally and very early, when he was still a beginning theology student listening to Ockham lecture. Such challenges would not have been out of place in this closed environment of elite young men, seeking by any means to distinguish themselves and to make a reputation. However, Chatton was an unusually tenacious and insightful critic, and his opposition to Ockham was not mere politics; it was quite fundamental, substantive, and long-lasting. We have no solid evidence that their personal relationship was acrimonious, but the debate was intense, frequently face-to-face, and it certainly had enough gravity to draw some of the next generation of Oxford thinkers into the fray on either side. For example, on the side of Ockham, Adam Wodeham (d. 1358), who was several years younger than Chatton, witnessed their exchanges and tended rather to line up against Chatton. In one documented incident, Wodeham was taking notes in attendance of one of Chatton's anti-Ockham lectures, and afterward rushed his copy-book to his mentor Ockham, revealing the latest positions from behind enemy lines. Ockham took the sheets from the young man and scribbled a philosophical reply to Chatton in Wodeham's margin. Wodeham himself related this story from his student days with pride, some years after the fact, in his *Sentences* commentary called *Lectura Secunda*, from the early 1330s.

The occasion of Ockham's first encounters with Chatton coincided with his initial expression of grand nominalism. In this same period Ockham began to see that his strategy required the razor to be fully sound; in short he began to see that some *independent* principle was needed for favoring the simpler ontology made possible by connotation theory over the richer ontology of realism. While it's unclear whether he realized this need exclusively as the result of criticism from Walter Chatton, it is clear that Ockham's recognition, articulation, and defense of the razor began just before 1319, and developed continually through many stages, under intense pressure from his critics (foremost Walter Chatton), up until around 1324. We also know that part of Chatton's response to this defense was to promulgate his own anti-razor, which will be discussed below.

Principles of Parsimony (and Plurality)

I say Ockham began a "recognition, articulation, and defense" of the razor at this time. I do not say that he *invented* the principle of Ockham's razor, for indeed he did not, despite the permanent link now existing between his name and this idea. Other important philosophers who have discussed this idea both before and after Ockham include Aristotle, who said "God and nature do nothing that is pointless" (*On the Heavens* I.4)—but also John Duns Scotus, Immanuel Kant (d. 1804), and W.V. Quine (d. 2000) have all advanced versions of their own. Modern interest in this principle continues unabated; philosophers, mathematicians, and scientists of all kinds are still fascinated by the meaning of and limits to this argument strategy.

Upon closer inspection we see not only that Ockham's razor has many supporters (and detractors), but also that there are in fact many substantially different razors. A more neutral term will sometimes be useful to capture the spirit of this broader genus, while allowing for further specification by different authors. The phrase 'principle of parsimony' seems to work well, and will be adopted in what follows. All parsimony principles have in common that they come down favorably on the question of *reduction*, and on the point of view that it is bad to have *too much*. But there is a very important distinction between different kinds of parsimony principles that it would be well to respect from the outset.

Some principles of parsimony are clearly meant to apply to the *world* and to *metaphysics*, while some are clearly meant to apply to *theories* and to *language*; there are those that say *reality* does not *in fact* have too much in it, and those that say our *theories* and explanations should not *posit* too much in them. For example, take the principle of parsimony we commonly hear in popular discourse today, roughly: 'All other things being equal, we should prefer the simpler theory.' This is a fine rule of thumb, and it is clearly a principle of parsimony, since it extols reduction. But notice that it does not attempt to make a claim about the nature of reality; all by itself it merely states that simpler theories are to be preferred. It does not attempt to tell us anything about what the world is actually like, only which theories of the world are best. By itself, such a razor is not committed to the view that the simplest theory is necessarily most accurate, or that reality itself is simple, but only that when choosing between theories otherwise equal, preferring the simpler one is rational. Let us classify this principle, and any others like it as *methodological principles of parsimony*, or as *methodological razors* for short, since they presume to tell us the correct method by which to select among otherwise attractive theories. Another example of a methodological razor is the claim 'the explanation with the simplest ontological commitments should be preferred'.

Now, by contrast, consider Aristotle's pronouncement above: 'God and nature do nothing that is pointless.' This is also a principle of parsimony, clearly. But it is not concerned with theory, and instead it makes direct claims about the nature of reality, or in other words, about metaphysics. It says that none of the products of nature and gods are useless or superfluous. Reality in fact contains no metaphysical extras. Notice, that by itself, this statement makes no claim about what theories of reality to prefer; rather it is aimed at reality directly. Since it is a claim about the nature of the world, let us classify this principle and others like it as *metaphysical principles of parsimony*, or as *metaphysical razors* for short, since they presume to tell us about the actual metaphysical simplicity of the world. Another example of a metaphysical razor is the claim 'every existing thing has a purpose'.

How do methodological and metaphysical razors relate to one another? There is no simple answer to this; it depends upon the content of what is claimed in each case. However, we can say generally that a metaphysical razor strongly suggests (or even perhaps entails) the corresponding methodological razor. For example, *if* you hold that god and nature do nothing that is pointless, *then* you will almost surely hold that the simplest theories of reality should be rationally preferred, on the added assumption that theories most likely to correspond to reality should be rationally preferred.

For if the universe, as a product of God and nature, is itself maximally simple, then if a theory is a model of the universe, then the simpler, the better (all else being equal).

However, the reverse implication does not hold; it does not follow from a belief that we should prefer the simpler theory that the universe itself is maximally simple. Indeed, there are many other reasons why simplicity might be preferred in a theoretical model, which reasons have nothing to do with how the world is: we might prefer a simpler theory because it is easier to manage, because it is easier to program into a computer, or because it is easier to quantify and subsume under mathematical methods. In fact, there are theories we prefer for certain uses today although we know they are false, because they are too simple: ideal gas laws, for example. Since some theories are only useful fictions, then although some such fictions are preferable to others on the basis of simplicity, we must admit there is no necessary connection between the utility of a theory and the structure of reality, and hence no methodological razor will in general give us sufficient grounds to accept its metaphysical counterpart. The important lesson for present purposes is that people committed to a metaphysical razor get a corresponding methodological razor for free, in fact they are practically stuck with it, but that those committed to a methodological razor can be more discerning; they can take or leave the corresponding metaphysical principle at their pleasure.

It is also useful at this stage to notice that principles of parsimony can have a kind of logical dual, which we could call *principles of plurality*, or, more colloquially, *anti-razors*. Such principles focus, not on avoiding too much, but rather on insuring that there is *enough*. Sometimes called "principles of plentitude" (for example by the Viennese-American mathematician, Karl Menger [d. 1985]), these principles tend to work with the opposite polarity of a razor. For example, the principle of plurality corresponding to Aristotle's razor—viz., 'God and nature do nothing that is pointless'—might be stated 'God and nature do nothing that is fruitless'. Reality has all that it needs, given the purposes of God and nature. This would be a *metaphysical principle of plurality*, extending the distinction we adopted above for razors, since this principle makes claims about reality. Similarly, we can imagine methodological plurality principles, say, 'all else being equal, prefer the theory with the most adequate ontology', or, 'prefer the richest theory'.

It might be assumed, given his reputation and the fact that a razor bears his name, that William Ockham propounded a parsimony principle, but not a plurality principle. It might also be guessed that this champion of nominalism held a metaphysical razor, thereby getting a methodological razor along in the bargain. To be specific, it might be assumed that Ockham held both that 'God and nature do nothing that is pointless' and that 'we should prefer the simplest explanation'; indeed, to judge from popular modern sources, the claim 'we should prefer the simplest explanation' just *is* Ockham's razor. (Go to any internet search engine, and type in 'Ockham's razor'; you will see hundreds of people claiming just this about Ockham and his razor. Try the French spelling 'Occam' and you will find still thousands more.)

However, all of the suppositions in the paragraph above are completely (and interestingly) false. Ockham actually held an anti-razor in addition to his razor; he never held any metaphysical razor that we know of, and in fact he argues explicitly that the metaphysical razor 'God and nature do nothing that is pointless' is *false*. Finally, as it turns out, the methodological razor 'prefer the simplest theory', while crudely capturing the *spirit* of Ockham's thought, nevertheless is not what Ockham really believed about parsimony. His actual views are far more subtle and rich. In the remainder of this chapter we sort fact from fiction, and see just what Ockham's razor is and what it is not, and also how his opponents received his views. Having sorted all this out, in the next chapter we will witness him argue in detail that there is no such thing as motion, by applying his real razor, together with connotation theory, as a one-two punch against the realist physicists of his day.

What Ockham's *Razor* Is

So, what is true about the real William of Ockham's real razor? First, Ockham never uses the term 'razor' or any similar word. He never wrote a little book called 'My Razor'; the term 'razor' seems to have been coined several hundred years after Ockham, although by whom is still controversial. So what did Ockham actually say that at least sounds like a razor (that is, like a parsimony principle)? Primarily this, from his commentary on the *Sentences*, which he was revising in the period we are now considering: "*Pluralitas non ponenda est sine necessitate,*" "A plurality should not be posited without necessity." But Ockham stated his razor principle differently at different times, for example:

1. "It is futile to do with more what can be done with fewer," in his *Treatise on Quantity*, from around 1323–24.

2. "When a proposition is made true for things, if two things suffice for its truth, it is superfluous to assume a third," in his *Quodlibet*, from around 1323–25.

Finally, his richest expression of the razor, and the one that exists in both his early and later works:

3. "No plurality should be assumed unless it can be proved (a) by reason, or (b) by experience, or (c) by some infallible authority," in his *Sentences* Commentary from around 1318–1319, in *Treatise on Quantity* from 1323–24, and in other places.

Despite the variety, Ockham experts have generally agreed, based on careful study of his writings, that the last formulation above gives the truest picture of Ockham's attitude toward parsimony. Using those same texts, we can fill out the three clauses with more precision, to obtain the following summary of his razor:

Ockham's Razor

No extra-mental distinction among extra-mental things should be assumed unless the distinction can be proved (a) by *arguments* from premises that are either self-evident or else come from indubitable experience or, (b) by unquestionable *experience* of extra-mental things, or (c) by some infallible *authority* such as the Bible, the Saints, or certain Ecclesiastical pronouncements.

Not very pithy. But it has the virtue of being based on Ockham's actual texts, and most importantly, examining it will yield great insight into Ockham's philosophical personality. Let us look at this summary at closer range, to clarify all the qualifications.

Overall, Ockham's razor has the form of an imperative about how we should conduct ourselves in making distinctions about extra-mental things, that is, things outside the mind—which is to say that Ockham is giving us advice on how to behave rationally when we wish to assume there are two things in the outside world instead of one, three things instead of two, and so forth. But notice that while we are given advice on the most rational method for generating rational distinctions in metaphysics, we are not thereby told anything about metaphysical reality itself. Consequently, Ockham's razor is a methodological principle, not a metaphysical one.

With the phrase *extra-mental distinction among extra-mental things*, Ockham just means he is talking about the right way to make real distinctions, as opposed to distinctions of mere reason. For example, comic book fans make a distinction of a sort between Superman and Clark Kent, but this distinction is merely mental. In using these distinct names, those of us privy to his secret identity do not intend any real distinction between the two; we know they are the same person. Ockham allows us to make as many of these merely mental distinctions as we find convenient and useful. Nor would he have in principle opposed invention and fiction; concepts can proliferate at pleasure within their own realm. But when we claim we are doing metaphysics about the external (= extra-mental) world, and so intend our distinctions to match up with reality, we need to invoke a much higher standard of evidence before we claim a putative distinction is real. How high? The three clauses set the bar: there are only three sources of evidence that are good enough to claim a real distinction exists: arguments, experience, and authority. Take them each in turn:

(a) *arguments from self-evident premises or premises of indubitable experience*—Ockham usually just uses the word *ratio* (= reason) for this clause, without further elaboration, intending of course that the arguments be of high logical strength. But he sometimes alters the formulation slightly by saying that we should not accept a given argument for positing a real distinction unless its premises are *known through themselves* (= *per se notae*), or, we might say today, *self-evident*. But this should probably not be interpreted too strictly. To the modern mind this might suggest Ockham claims that only conceptual knowledge can form the starting points of sound reasoning about distinctions, but this is not correct. All he has in mind is that we ought not to posit a new entity if there is serious rational disagreement on the matter: we ought to posit a distinctly new entity only when the matter is argumentatively without substantive controversy. To remind us that empirical premises can also give us a good reason to form a distinction, provided they are uncontroversial, I favor adding the qualifier 'premises of indubitable experience'.

(b) *unquestionable experience of extra-mental things*—If, as per (a), we should trust conclusions drawn from premises based on indubitable experience, quite obviously we should also trust indubitable experience itself. This clause shows clearly how negligibly philosophical skepticism shaped Ockham's intellectual temperament. Modern philosophers might object that no philosophical distinction should be held to such a standard, since no experience is indubitable, and that the best we can do is to build a reasonable and coherent theory of our (always doubtable) experiences. But this level of anxiety about skepticism is alien to Ockham's mind. For this reason, although the similarity tempts many philosophers, Ockham should not be compared too closely with the skeptically-minded American nominalist W.V. Quine, who believed we have no theory-neutral access to the external world, and so rejected the very idea of indubitable experience, asserting in his own methodological razor that we should manage the ontology of our network of beliefs with an eye to simplicity. In short, Quine's razor, unlike Ockham's, really was just 'prefer the simpler theory, all else being equal'.

Here the study of Ockham's actual razor affords its deepest insight into what is different about his philosophical temperament. While for Quine and many who follow him, all physical objects are mere postulates, best-guesses that could all be wrong—atoms, Homer's gods, and tables and chairs are all just postulates we invent and use to navigate the world of experience—for Ockham physical objects are real extra-mental things, the structure of which he is willing to describe in terms of some Aristotelian theoretical concepts (substance and quality), but not others (relation, quantity, motion, universal essences, and so on). As a result, Ockham believed in substance and quality and not in relations and motion, but is not at all for the same reasons he believed in his own bed, say. Ockham follows a kind of direct realism about the external world, assuming that human beings normally have reliable access to an objective world independent from their inner cognitive life.

In consequence of these attitudes, Quine eschewed most metaphysics as bad science, and as a skeptic about the external world could assert no metaphysical razor, only a methodological one, since we don't really *know* what the external world is like; by contrast, Ockham thought that metaphysics *is* science, wanted it to be done well, and as a theologian and a direct realist asserted a methodological razor, but could not subscribe to a metaphysical razor for religious reasons, to be discussed in the next section. Despite the temptation to see the situation otherwise, as clause (b) shows, these two men's nominalism could not be more different foundationally, and simply lumping them both together as 'nominalists' who advocate '*the* razor' (as if there were only one) glosses profound differences of outlook.

(c) *some infallible authority*—Ockham has in mind the authority of religious texts and figures: the Bible, the pronouncements of saints and fathers of the church, and also ecclesiastical pronouncements. Most people have no idea that this is part of the razor, but Ockham gives equal weight to religion, reason and experience as a legitimate cause for making a metaphysical distinction.

We already have seen an example of clause (c) in action: the attack on the category of RELATION. We cannot see relations—for example, we do not directly experience some Aristotelian entity fatherhood—nor does reason support the existence of such entities, since connotation theory can explain the truth of propositions such as 'Socrates is the father of two sons' or 'Fatherhood is a relation' perfectly well without needing to posit the entity fatherhood as the realist does. Consequently, the razor would suggest that we be rid of the category altogether, *but for the church's teaching that fatherhood is real in the trinity*. This is enough of a reason for Ockham to posit fatherhood in the trinity as an entity distinct from the three persons in the trinity itself; to use the technical language of theology, there is a real metaphysical distinction between fatherhood and God the Father. By contrast, since we can explain the truth of propositions containing the term 'similarity' using connotation theory and other semantic devices, and since the church and direct experience say nothing about the existence of similarity, none of the three clauses (a), (b), or (c) is satisfied, and so the razor demands that we do not posit similarity as something really distinct from the individual substances that happen to be similar to each other.

Ockham's Razor and Chatton's Anti-Razor

This last example, in which this entity is posited but that entity is not, suggests that Ockham believed the three clauses above could be used both positively and negatively, that is, both to determine when we should posit a distinction (when at least one of the clauses is met), and also when we should not posit a distinction (when none of the clauses are met). But since razors only have the negative function, it seems we have discovered that Ockham also intended the three clauses of his complex principle of parsimony to function positively as a principle of plurality, or anti-razor, when turned around:

Ockham's Anti-Razor

An extra-mental distinction among extra-mental things should be assumed if the distinction can be proved (a) either by arguments from self-evident premises or from premises of indubitable experience or, (b) by unquestionable experience of extra-mental things, or (c) by some infallible authority such as the Bible, the Saints, or certain Ecclesiastical pronouncements.

In the examples on page 98 above, the three clauses exert both positive and negative functions, telling fellow philosopher-theologians they *must* posit the relation <u>fatherhood</u> (anti-razor) in the Trinity but that they *may not* posit the relation <u>similarity</u> (razor).

Walter Chatton, whom we met above, doubted the power of Ockham's anti-razor and its application in certain instances, and he fundamentally opposed Ockham's constant reliance on the razor. Nor was he alone historically in insisting that razors need a robust counter-balancing force to insure they don't cut away too much, a powerful way of arguing *for* distinction and plurality to balance against the reductive power of a razor. Kant also believed in the need for vigorous anti-razors; in the *Critique of Pure Reason* he claims that an equal regulative principle of reason was needed to balance out a razor.

In order to show Ockham how anti-razors were needed, and how a realist anti-razor would work, Chatton invented and advanced his own anti-razor throughout the 1320s. Here are a few different phrasings of Chatton's anti-razor:

1. Where an affirmative proposition is verified for things, if fewer things . . . aren't sufficient, one must posit more.

2. Consider an affirmative proposition, which, when it is verified, is verified only for things; if three things do not suffice for the purpose of verifying it, one has to posit a fourth, and so on in turn [for four things, or five, and so on].

3. Likewise, there is a sufficient necessity for positing three things, when (a) a proposition is verified for things, and (b) two things, howsoever they are present without another thing, are not sufficient for the truth of the proposition.

This third version is the most complicated, and needs to be explained. Chatton liked to use his anti-razor as a kind of meditation on ontology. Take a proposition that we know is true—say we're successfully lighting a charcoal barbecue with a match, then it is true that 'This flame lights these coals'. What must be real in order for this proposition to be true? Not just the flame and the coals, as Ockham would say, but also a relational entity <u>heating</u> in the flame and another such entity, <u>being heated</u> in the coals, says Chatton. The reason is this: if we imagine that nothing exists, and then imagine that only the flame existed and the coals existed, it would not immediately imply that 'This flame lights these coals'; if you just strike a match and stand there with it, not touching the coals, no relation exists and so the flame does nothing to the coals. More than simply existing, the two items must interact somehow in order for 'This flame lights these coals' to be true. But this interaction is explained in the Aristotelian system as a pair of accidents, <u>heating</u> in the flame, <u>being heated</u> in the coals, which entities are in the categories of ACTION and PASSION. Hence, in order to explain the truth of 'This flame lights these coals' we must posit real causal relations according to reason, whereas Ockham thought reason would not lead us to posit causal relations. In this way Chatton used his principle of plurality to try to resurrect some branches of the tree of beings so sadly pruned by the sharp edge of Ockham's razor.

Ockham's razor forms a very natural coupling with its corresponding anti-razor; the same three clauses tell me when to posit and when not to posit. But Ockham's razor alone, with the background of connotation theory, does not consistently couple with Chatton's anti-razor, since Ockham's anti-razor requires us to posit relations in the Trinity and nowhere else, while Chatton's forces us to posit other relations in the natural world as well. Nevertheless, some people have insisted generally, without careful thinking, that 'razors and anti-razors are two sides of the same coin', merely two ways of looking at the same idea, which is this: have exactly the right ontology. The razor says, 'not too much', the anti-razor 'make sure you have enough'. But this simple view can no longer satisfy us, as if there were only one razor and one anti-razor in the world. In fact, different razors and anti-razors can conflict in content. True, *some* anti-razors are the opposite side of *certain* razors, as in we saw with Ockham's razor and anti-razor, based on one and the same trio of clauses. But this does not mean that any arbitrarily chosen razor and anti-razor are complementary or even consistent with each other.

Putting Ockham's razor and his anti-razor together, it appears that he actually held an all-in-one principle of parsimony and plurality based on his three clauses. If we call such all-in-one principles *rules of rational positing*, then we have discovered:

Ockham's Rule of Rational Positing

An extra-mental distinction among extra-mental things should be assumed if and only if the distinction can be proved (a) either by arguments from self-evident premises or from premises of indubitable experience or, (b) by unquestionable experience of extra-mental things, or (c) by some infallible authority such as the Bible, the Saints, or certain Ecclesiastical pronouncements.

The thrust of this rule is that we ought to have the highest standards—rational, experiential, and religious—when making distinctions in metaphysics, and that any one of these sources is sufficient on its own to make such distinctions. This general rule having been discovered, we must still admit that William Ockham applied the razor with greater relish than the anti-razor, and that the general direction of his thought was toward reduction, in other words toward parsimony, and as Chapter 4 showed, it was on ontological reduction that he spent the majority of his time and energy.

Modern Misunderstandings: What *Ockham's* Razor Is Not

Many myths about Ockham's razor surface from time to time in general intellectual culture. We are now in a position to go a little deeper into the issues, including an examination and rejection of the two most interesting and widespread such myths.

Myth #1: Ockham's Razor Is Anti-Religious

A famous story tells that French scientist Pierre-Simon Laplace (d. 1827) was once asked by Napoleon why his book on celestial mechanics contained no reference to God, the very author of the celestial realm, and of all else besides. Quipped Laplace: "I have no need of that hypothesis." When many people think of Ockham's razor they think of it in this way, as trimming needless hypotheses, wielded specifically against theism and in favor of naturalism. The following anecdote illustrates concretely this strong tendency.

While browsing a bookstore one day I found a large, fiery-red hardback with library binding which called itself *Who's Who in Hell: A Handbook and International Directory for Humanists, Freethinkers, Naturalists, Rationalists, and Non-Theists*, by Warren Allen Smith. The book gives brief and not unamusing biographies of people who had courageously advanced the cause of reason in the face of religious irrationalism, and who (tongue in cheek) had paid for this with eternal damnation (ruled over no doubt by Milton's Satan!) Drawn in by the intriguing title I flipped through a few pages and was quite surprised to see the author had listed Brother William Ockham among the denizens of Tartarus. Ockham's short entry did not say whether Smith regarded him as a humanist, freethinker, naturalist, rationalist, or non-theist, but he did specify that Ockham had earned his place with Hume and Galileo by espousing the razor and defying the pope. No doubt he must have had in mind something like the remark of Laplace above; Ockham said that we should prefer the simplest theory, but physical theories of the universe which do not invoke God have efficacy and are simpler than theistic theories; hence modern people no longer have need of that postulate.

Whatever we may think of this line of reasoning, it is an easy matter to see that *Ockham's* razor says no such thing, and that if he really is in hell for the razor, he has earned his infernal sinecure for nothing. For, if we apply his rule of rational positing from above, we see immediately that clause (c) requires the philosopher-theologian to posit God as distinct from creation, since the Bible and other authorities demand it.

This example shows how *situated* Ockham was in his own world; in his philosophy we find no recognition of other religions, of non-theistic religion, or of atheistic philosophy. He was not concerned to make his views accessible to a secular audience, but to defeat the claims of rival Christian philosopher-theologians. Despite modern attempts to paint him otherwise, and to reclaim him for the tastes of a modern, pluralistic, and secular culture in which such older attitudes are (rightly) seen as unworkable, William Ockham simply was not secular or pluralistic (or modern!).

MYTH #2: IN HIS RAZOR OCKHAM ASSUMED THAT THE WORLD IS MAXIMALLY SIMPLE

Often people fail to distinguish methodological and metaphysical razors, and so in effect assume that anyone committed to simpler theories does so *based on* the conviction that the world is maximally simple. But as we have seen, although metaphysical razors as good as imply corresponding methodological ones, methodological razors can be held without subscribing to metaphysical ones. Since Ockham's razor is methodological, he had his choice about whether to believe the world is maximally simple or not, in other words about whether God and nature do nothing pointlessly.

Although he would not hold that God ever acts *pointlessly*, Ockham did hold very clearly in his revised *Sentences* commentary, Book I, that God made more things than he needed to. Here are his own words, translated by Marilyn Adams:

> There are many things that God does with more that He could do with fewer. Nor should any other explanation be sought. And it follows from the fact that He wills it that it is fitting and not futile for it to be done. (*William Ockham*, Volume 1, p. 159)

We could not ask for a clearer statement of his position on the corresponding metaphysical razor. It is false. The universe is not maximally simple. What did God make that is 'extra', according to Ockham? Probably he has in mind the Christian plan of salvation; God made provision for salvation of humanity even thought he did not have to do so. But there might be even more to it than this.

For if we think about it clearly, no Christian—indeed, no one who accepts the doctrine of creation—can possibly accept a razor that says 'God made no more than he had to make'. For consider, if God created freely, he did not have to create anything at all—there isn't anything that God had to make; but then if there isn't anything that God had to make, then if he didn't make anything that he didn't have to make, then he wouldn't have made anything. *Every created thing* is in a sense superfluous according to the doctrine of creation. Nevertheless, no medieval theologian would say that God created *pointlessly*, and Ockham is very explicit in the quotation above that he believes God, although perfectly wise and good, made things which violate Aristotle's metaphysical razor, things which are in some sense *too much*.

The lesson is as simple as it is fascinating: we should never let anyone tell us that Ockham's razor means 'nature is perfectly simple, therefore the simpler our theories the better'. This principle might be a good one. But this is quite evidently not what Ockham meant.

Medieval Misunderstandings: Ordained versus Absolute Power

In the discussion of these modern myths we have seen the way certain razors can have (or not have) theological implications. In Ockham's own time, as his razor and his grand nominalism became more popular, more discussed, and more controversial, Ockham's clarifications of them went further and further afield, until he began to touch on important contemporary debates in theology about simplicity in nature, creation, and divine power. Hence, although Ockham rejected metaphysical razors out of hand, it is worth taking a deeper look at some possible interpretations of the doctrine of creation to see precisely where the conflicts with metaphysical razors actually lie, with special reference to Ockham's views on this subject. As we will see, the issue turns out to be theologically explosive, and will afford a glimpse into why Ockham's views eventually came under direct ecclesiastical condemnation.

In order to begin, we need a distinction and a simple example of how one might try to make a razor fit with the doctrine of creation. Let us assume the basic idea of a creator God. Then, we can talk about: (1) the entire universe, and think of it as a system God created as a whole, or, alternatively, we can focus on (2) the elements or parts of that system. Given this difference, we should be clear: as I argued above, the doctrine of creation says that God did not have to create *the system of reality as a whole*. This immediately entails that God did not have to create *any element within the system either*, of course. However, it is possible to use this distinction to be more refined, and to claim the following razor: given that God has a certain purpose for the whole system, each element in the system also has a purpose, and so is not superfluous, extra, or too much. So by using this distinction, it is consistent with the doctrine of creation to assert a razor which says that although the system as a whole is (absolutely) superfluous, nevertheless each part of it has a (relative) purpose.

In the early 1320s, when Ockham got into trouble at Oxford for some of his theology, it was in part because of the way he used a very similar theological distinction which goes back to Scotus (and even linguistically to Aquinas, who nevertheless interpreted it differently). Ockham distinguished God's *absolute power* on the one hand—that is, the fact that God could set up any world system he liked or none at all, and could then interact with this system at will—from God's *ordained power* on the other—that is, the fact that God can act within the specific system he has created, given that it has already been chosen and created with certain general laws in place. Using this distinction, Ockham claimed that when God acts within the world order he acts by his ordained power, but when he acts by his power to circumvent the very order he created, he then acts by his absolute power. For example, God could, by absolute power, have made a world where gravity had less force than it actually does, say half as much. In such a world, people on Earth could easily jump ten feet into the air unaided. So, absolutely speaking God could have made it possible that human beings jump ten feet into the air by having made a different world from the outset. However, given the world God actually made, can God make it that human beings jump ten feet into the air? Well, yes and no: (1) he can still do so absolutely, provided he undermines the law of gravity that he himself originally made, that is, God could accomplish this change, but this would be miraculous, not natural; (2) viewed from the point of view of the ordered system he created, God cannot do so, since this would violate that system. So the answer to 'Can God make it that human beings are able to jump ten feet into the air?' would be 'yes, by his absolute power, but no, by his ordained power'.

Or again, by his absolute power God could have made a world without gravity at all, which nevertheless behaves just as our world does, if, for example, he alone were to constantly cause masses to attract each other by Newton's inverse square law. By contrast, suppose God wants to make St. Paul fall from his horse to the ground on the way to Damascus he doesn't have to be fancy about it; he can do so by keeping gravity as he originally made it, and, say, hitting the horse and then letting gravity do the rest. We would say this is according to God's ordained power. But presumably God could have got Paul's attention by making him just exist on the ground instantly, or by making him hover in midair, or some by other unnatural method. However, this would be by absolute, not ordained power. Theologically, it seems this distinction is really between God as creator and supernatural actor in history, versus God as natural agent in history.

Now, with these distinctions at our command, let us list several distinct metaphysical razors, and for each one ask: (a) Does this razor conflict with the doctrine of creation? (b) Would Ockham agree with this razor, and if not why not? The razors are listed in increasing order of subtlety and theological danger:

Metaphysical Razor 1: Every element of reality is necessary in the sense that God was bound to make it.
a) Obviously conflicts with the doctrine of creation.
(b) Ockham would therefore reject it.

Metaphysical Razor 2: God did not make anything he did not have to make.
a) Clearly conflicts with the doctrine of creation, as shown on page 000 above, since God did not have to make anything at all.
(b) Ockham would therefore reject it.

Metaphysical Razor 3: Out of all the possible systems of reality God could have made, he in fact made the simplest one, that is, the one with the smallest number of categories of reality.

(a) No conflict with the doctrine of creation.

(b) Ockham rejects it. We saw an unambiguous quotation denying this claim; I speculated that he thinks salvation is superfluous (but important and merciful, of course).

So far, everything is clear. But now consider:

> *Metaphysical Razor 4*: God has definite purposes for every element of reality, (even if human beings don't know what they are).
>
> (a) No conflict with the doctrine of creation, if we distinguish the system and its elements (or God's absolute versus ordained power) as above. Every element can have ordained necessity but still be superfluous when taken individually and absolutely, or even when taken as a whole. We can consistently hold that in fact God ordained a rational system of elements in which each part has purpose, but that he is not beholden absolutely to any element, or to the system as a whole, and so retains his absolute power.
>
> (b) Ockham would probably accept this razor on religious grounds. And since Ockham believed in the distinction between ordained and absolute power, for him this razor is consistent with the doctrine of creation.

This highlights the philosophical usefulness of the doctrine of ordained and absolute power. But now consider the really difficult case, a more elaborated version of Razor 4:

> *Metaphysical Razor 5*: Every element of reality is necessary in the sense of being needed to accomplish some goal God has.
>
> (a) This does not conflict with the doctrine of creation, if we distinguish ordained and absolute power, but it does suggest some dependency of God on creatures, in that God needs creatures to accomplish some of his goals.
>
> (b) From Ockham's point of view this formulation goes too far back toward Razors 1 and 2, and is unacceptable. Ockham explicitly says it is false that God needs creatures to

accomplish his goals. God can do directly *anything* that he
does using a creature as an intermediary.

Ockham's attitude toward Razor 5 here might surprise us, but in
fact it has a historical as well as a philosophical basis.

It might look as if anyone holding the distinction between
ordained and absolute power could just respond to Razor 5 as they
did to Razor 4, because, as we saw in the example of one-half gravity, the idea of ordained power seems to imply that, given certain
initial divine choices, God afterward has certain (self-imposed)
limits in dealing with the creation; having made gravity at such-
and-such a level he must change or override gravity in order to
make things different. Once created, gravity must be *dealt with* as
such, even by God, although he need not have made gravity in the
first place. The problem is that this last claim comes dangerously
close to conflicting with the doctrine of divine omnipotence. Why
should the omnipotent creator of gravity have to deal with gravity
to get things done? Moreover, just by the very name, 'the distinction between God's ordained and absolute power' it sounds as if
God has two distinct powers, not one, and so is not metaphysically
simple. And in short, this distinction and its possible application to
the acceptance of Razor 5 seems poised to conflict with items (4)
and (5) (the doctrine of creation and divine omnipotence, respectively) from our Top Ten List of Christian Doctrines in Chapter 2.
But this would make the distinction quite heretical.

As might be expected, when Ockham elaborated the distinction
between ordained and absolute power, and especially when he
applied it to the theological question of grace and salvation, this
pair of dangerous implications was spotted immediately by his enemies, and he was reported to church authorities. Ockham tried to
explain himself, and to counter the charges by clarifying his views
in various ways, for example, by (in effect) distinguishing cases like
Razor 4 from cases like Razor 5. Ockham affirmed under this pressure that God does not need creatures to accomplish any of his
goals, and can do directly anything that he does using a creature as
an intermediary. But this backdoor attempt to reaffirm God's
omnipotence and his own orthodoxy was not fully believed, and he
was forced to stress it so often that it left him open to the charge
that he believed God can do anything *no matter how whimsical or
arbitrary*, for example, that a person living a perfect Christian life,

loving God and taking all the sacraments, could nevertheless be sent to hell by God in his absolute power!

This was not exactly Ockham's view of course, but his keenness to discuss razors and simplicity, together with his tendency to accept the distinction between ordained and absolute power, left him open to this charge by his enemies. It is on account of this misunderstanding that, to this very day, Ockham is sometimes touted as a precursor to the Reformation. After all, he seemed to claim for God a kind of absolute power over salvation, thereby implying a concomitant reduction in the importance of priests and sacraments, just as Martin Luther himself would eventually do explicitly almost two hundred years later.

Sliding from Nominalism to Heresy?

Official charges were not filed until 1323, and the process of examining him for heresy moved slowly; it was not until 1324 that Ockham was finally called to Avignon to explain himself to Pope John XXII, and only in 1326 was he (mostly) cleared of the charges; his ideas were censured but not condemned. However, it is important to see that Ockham's troubling ideas began back here, around 1319–1321.

There is some evidence to suggest that the motives of those who turned Ockham in (more on this in Chapter 7) were partly personal. For example, not everyone at Oxford agreed with Ockham about whether to reject a principle such as Razor 5; some in fact accepted it. And yet, although Ockham rejected views such as Razor 5 in part to *get out* of trouble, not everyone who would have openly accepted Razor 5 thereby got himself *into* trouble. Without finding themselves subsequently in any danger, some Oxonians upheld the absolute/ordained distinction and asserted, albeit carefully, that there are some things that God cannot do without creatures. For example, God cannot make Socrates the father of Plato if there is no Socrates. Or to take a modern example, God cannot make a Picasso painting; only Picasso can. God can make any painting Picasso can make, to be sure, there is no question of skill, but without Picasso, any painting God made wouldn't really be a Picasso painting. And although this view might very well seem to conflict *logically* with divine omnipotence, from a *psychological* point of view it is in fact more easily reconcilable with orthodoxy, since it suggests that, given that God set up a certain system of salvation (with priests, sacraments, and so forth) he has to stick to that system. Foremost among the thinkers who 'got away with' accepting the ordained/absolute distinction in such a manner contrary to Ockham was the Franciscan theology student we met in this chapter, Friar Walter Chatton.

Let us briefly summarize the two-fold source of Ockham's strange slide from nominalism to alleged heresy. First, he simply angered a great many realists; his attempt to use the razor to make his connotation theory rationally required instead of merely optional ultimately suggested that much of the theologically-based, speculative theological metaphysics of his day was unsound and irrational. Second, in seeking to advance and to validate his views on language, Ockham gave controversial opinions on metaphysics; which in turn required clarification and defense of his razor from people like Chatton; which in turn required distinctions that impacted divine omnipotence and the doctrine of creation. Starting with language, Ockham had wandered into the metaphysical and theological minefield described above, the navigation of which would ultimately prove greater than his resources.

In response he attempted to blunt the force of Chatton's repeated counter-attacks by trying to show exactly how his grand nominalism worked on a theologically neutral subject: the case of motion. Using connotation theory and the razor, Ockham proposed a radical theory of motion, and an astonishingly minimalist account of physics generally. Possibly he sought to divert attention from his more controversial theological views about divine power and salvation. But if so, it did not work. In fact, arguably, it made things worse, because this elaboration on motion sharpened his razor to an even finer edge, and thereby increased the sense of danger his realist opponents felt from its reductive power. His remarkable views on motion and physics, to which we will next turn, were the last philosophical issues he would be able tackle relatively unmolested by ecclesiastical politics.

6

The Teacher Responds
(1321–1323)
Physics and Motion

Despite the biographical uncertainty that sometimes restricts our understanding of the stages of medieval debates, we do have one clear fixed point in Ockham's life during this period: wherever he was living, whether London or Oxford, he was living among a group of Franciscan friars that included Walter Chatton, and he was responding, sometimes daily, to the attacks Chatton made against him. The constant pressure to correct misperceptions of (and genuine resistance to) his views, fueled by Chatton's unending attacks, forced Ockham to explore the further and further the consequences of his nominalism.

One direction that Ockham's response took was a further investigation outside of theology proper, into natural philosophy, or as we call it today, physics. Between 1322 and 1324 he composed three different books on natural philosophy, including a large commentary on Aristotle's *Physics*. Probably none of this activity was strictly necessary for his career, that is, none of this activity was required for a degree in theology. We can speculate that he wrote for intellectual pleasure, to further clarify and defend his metaphysical views, and to busy himself producing non-theological texts, hoping perhaps that some of the controversy would die down. However, with Ockham this response was bound to be vigorous, original, and obdurate, and it only deepened the ire of his contemporaries even further.

In fact, the scientific implications of his razor still tend to shock modern people. For Ockham argued very forcefully that the razor, properly applied, would cut away <u>motion</u> from reality. There really are moving things, things changing location, *but there really is no such thing as motion.* Moreover, physics, which many regard as the science of motion, a body of knowledge about motion taking place in the external world, is not this after all, according to Ockham; since motion is unreal and since science is about the real, physics cannot be about motion. Strictly speaking no *external* inquiry into motion is possible; instead, *physics is ultimately about our internal (but objective) concepts about motion, and the true mental proposi- tions such terms compose.*

To understand his arguments for these amazing conclusions, worked out and written down in either London or Oxford, we first must talk about how motion was explained by realists, how Ockham criticized the realist theories, and then how, using con- notation theory, he argued for its elimination altogether. We will then be able finally to critique Ockham's grand nominalism not at a general, programmatic level, but rather at the level of a particu- lar concrete application. We can then complete our examination of Ockham's ontology by examining the strange account of physics his ontology forced him to give. And in fact, this theory of physics is one of the last pieces of non-political philosophy he developed before the absolute/ordained controversy caught up with him.

The Aristotelian View of Motion and the Science of Motion (= Physics)

It is best to begin with one or two points about the Aristotelian background of the late medieval discussion of physics, especially the introduction of a few pieces of terminology. Today we use the term 'motion' to refer only to a certain kind of change, that is, the change that happens when an object changes *location*. In the medieval discussions, by contrast, the word 'motion' is completely synonymous with 'change'; that is, it has much broader significa- tion than we give it today. For example, when a colorful shirt is hung outside too long and is bleached out by the sun, it becomes pale; Aristotle would call this movement from colorful to pale 'motion'. If it were then wadded up and tossed into the trash, this change of location would also be called 'motion'. But obviously these are very different types of motion or change. Because 'motion' had wider signification, medieval people needed a way to refer to the kind of motion that occurs when things change loca- tion; the term 'local motion' was chosen for obvious reasons, and we still use the term 'locomotion' in English to this day. The upshot is twofold. (1) When Ockham discusses motion, he sometimes intends the term broadly, as we use the word 'change'. (2) To keep things straight, the different kinds of motion or change had special names:

1. change of location   [such as a falling rock] = *local motion*

2. change of quality   [such as colorful → pale] = *alteration*

3. quantitative change [such as gaining weight] = *growth* or *decay*

4. essential becoming   [such as being born] = *generation*

5. essential destruction [such as dying] = *corruption* or *destruction*

In line with modern usage, this chapter will use 'motion' as a synonym for 'local motion', so long as no confusion results, but when more precision is needed the terms 'local motion', 'alteration', and so on, will be used.

As this chart (and our discussion of Aristotelian philosophy in Chapter 2) suggest, there are two kinds of motion/change:

(a) *Substantial change or essential change.* This is when a primary substance, say Socrates, comes into being (generation) or passes out of being (corruption). When a thing of type X undergoes substantial change, it becomes either X-for-the-first-time (generation) or becomes no-longer-X (corruption). These changes are covered by categories 4 and 5 above.

(b) *Accidental change.* This is when a primary substance takes on or looses a non-essential property. These changes are covered by categories 1–3 above. For example, when Socrates falls asleep or wakes up, when he is wearing shoes or is barefoot, when he shrinks as he ages, when he is heated by the sun or cools himself with a fan, when he changes places by walking around the agora, when he stands on his head, and in short, when he changes in any of the nine accidental categories, he undergoes accidental change.

No matter the variety of change we are talking about—whether accidental or essential, creative or destructive—Aristotle tended to analyze change as a shift from one state of affairs (such as being colorful) to a contrary or contradictory state of affairs (such as being pale) brought about by a causal agent (such as the sun) in some underlying thing that does not itself change but instead receives the change (the shirt). Or more schematically, all change is a movement from **contrary$_1$** to **contrary$_2$** in a **substrate**, brought about by an **agent** (= **efficient cause**). Hence, there are four *distinct* principles to any change:

1. the way a thing is before the change [= **contrary$_1$**]

2. the way a thing is after the change [= **contrary$_2$**]

3. that which underlies the change [= **substrate**]

4. the agent of the change [= **efficient cause**]

This is quite easy to understand in the case of accidental changes; the example of the bleached-out shirt easily fits this pattern. Or again, if I lose twenty pounds, then this change of quantity is from one state of affairs (my original weight)[1] to another state of affairs (my original weight minus 20) in a substrate (me) caused by an agent (my willful reduction of calories). Thus the substrate in accidental change is almost always an individual substance, such as this man, or this shirt, or this magnolia tree. The substrate of essential change is harder to explain; the medievals often interpreted Aristotle as saying that the substrate of all essential change is matter (sometimes called 'prime matter'). Since prime matter has no substantial form (after all, its job is to be the stable, underlying thing that receives substantial forms) it is not a 'this something', and so not a substance in any ordinary sense. It is pure, undetermined potentiality.

The Mediaeval Realists' Theory of Local Motion

Both Ockham and his medieval opponents believed in the same basic Aristotelian picture of change as described above; that is,

---

[1] I'm not telling.

their disagreement about local motion takes place in the Aristotelian framework. But, as always, the medieval realist takes some liberties with his ancient sources. Putting together the ideas explained above, and taking a somewhat literal view of the notion that if something makes a difference to truth it must be real, medieval realists would say that:

> Local motion is a form of accidental change imparted to an individual substance (which substance acts as the substratum for the change), in which the potential to move is reduced to actuality via the moving agent by the acquisition of a new accidental form in the thing moved, which form we will write as <u>motion</u>; the acquisition of such a form is the immediate reason why anything moves.

To distill this down to a definition, the realists would say that:

> X is moving = $_{DF}$ X has acquired from its mover an accident, <u>motion</u>, which causes X to undergo change of location.

Basically their explanation works like this. In the instant a thing begins to move, it acquires from the agent that moves it a real thing, <u>motion</u>, which thing is a successive accident inhering in the permanent moving object. (A *permanent* entity is something fully present in every instant of its existence, such as an ox, whereas a *successive* entity is one that does not have its whole being present in an instant, such as a day.) When the object ceases to move, it loses this accident. When a sentence of the form 'X is in motion' is true it is because this accident inheres in X; when 'X is in motion' is false it is because the accident does not inhere in X. Thus, at any given instant that a thing remains in motion, its motion is explained by the possession of this accident.

The metaphysics here is robust and simple. Motion is a real thing. There is a perfectly respectable place for motion in Aristotelian philosophy; it is an accident. So, the realist thinks, when the physicist studies s given motion, he is studying a real part of the world, to wit, the accidental form <u>motion</u>: how it is imparted, how it is sustained, how it is intensified or weakened. Physics is a science of real things, and in particular physics studies the form of motion and its consequences. The picture here is not crazy; it seems consistent and reasonable in many ways. The pre-supposition is that propositions get to be true or false based on what things exist or not. This is called 'the principle of contradictories', and it underlies many realist arguments in metaphysics; if a proposition changes *truth value*, that is from false to true or true to false, then some element of reality came into being or went out of being, causing this to happen. The principle is sometimes stated like this:

> It is impossible for contradictory propositions to be successively verified for one and the same thing, except on account of the production or destruction of some real thing.

In particular, this principle underlies the realist position about the cause of motion and the subject matter of physics. Since all forms of motion (local, alteration, and so on) are real changes, described by propositions which change truth value accordingly (for instance, 'This shirt is colorful' is first true, then false), it must be that something has come into or gone out of existence (for example, the accidental color forms first exist in the shirt, then they leave). Since these real things are making a difference to truth, these real forms would obviously be the real objects of any scientific study of change, and this means a real form of <u>motion</u> is the real object of the science of local motion, viz., physics.

Ockham's Rejection

However, Ockham, who as we have seen applies a greater subtlety to the question of how propositions get to be true or false, rejects this whole picture. To get a complete sense of his views, we must consider four aspects of Ockham's rejection:

(1) How did he argue against this realist theory of motion?

(2) What explanation does he offer of the meaning of the word 'motion', and of the truth conditions of sentences like 'X is moving'?

(3) What explanation does he offer of the phenomenon of moving things?

(4) How does he explain what the science of physics is about,
if it's not about motion?

Anti-Realism and Ockham's Alternative

The account I will develop here is drawn from Ockham's
Quodlibet, a record of seven live debate sessions he conducted
from 1322 to 1324. In particular, I take these ideas from the earliest such session we have, *Quodlibet* I, question 5, from 1322,
right in the middle the phase of his life we are currently considering. In that text, Ockham held that <u>motion</u> is not an element of
the world separable from other things. Local motion does not sub-
sist or have being of its own. It is, strictly speaking, unreal. Things
move locally, but there is no accidental form <u>motion</u> *per se*. His
argument against motion is simple, and is based on God's absolute
power. If motion were a thing distinct from permanent things,
then it would be possible for God, who can do anything that is
logically possible by his absolute power, to preserve <u>motion</u> and
destroy all permanent entities. That is, God could preserve <u>motion</u>
and destroy everything else. So <u>motion</u> could exist, and yet *there
would exist no moving things*. Moreover, if <u>motion</u> were a thing distinct from permanent things, as the realists would have it, then
God could also preserve all things, even moving things, and
destroy <u>motion</u>. But then things would move even though the
accident <u>motion</u> no longer existed.

Moreover, the realist's arguments from language—if we have a
word 'motion' that occurs in true sentences then there must be a
real, independent entity corresponding to it—does not force us to
accept the existence of such an entity. If we regard the term
'motion' as connotative, and construct a theory of moving things
based on this hypothesis, then the linguistic impetus to say motion
is an independent thing evaporates, since 'motion' will have a
nominal definition, and not a real definition.

Hence, for Ockham, motion is simply a term—merely a word.
In fact, it is a connotative term, primarily signifying a moving
object and secondarily signifying that this object exists in the following manner: (1) successively, in different places, (2) without
intervening rest, and (3) continuously. Ockham adds the third
clause to account for a case where God would destroy X, then create it again in another place; this would fit (1) and (2), but no one

would call it local motion. Since 'motion' is a connotative term, it has a nominal definition, which is captured by the three clauses above. Hence, in brief, Ockham's definition of motion is:

X is in motion $=_{\text{NDF}}$ X successively coexists in different places, without intervening rest, continuously.

Or, look at the matter from the point of view of truth values. Essentially, Ockham analyzes a sentence like 'X is in motion' as 'X is in a place at time t, and at $t^* \neq t$, X is (continuously, without rest) in another place'. Or again, most simply: 'X is in motion' means 'X is here and at another time there, and X hits every point in between here and there without stopping on the way'. Notice that on this account, motion is analyzed in terms of two distinct instants of time, that is, in terms of a *passage of time* over an interval. This lapse of time is an absolutely essential element of the analysis, since X cannot be in two distinct places (both here and there) at the *same* instant. Ockham is here relying on an expanded version of the principle of contradictories, which he stated in his *Sentences* commentary as follows:

> It is impossible for contradictories [i.e., contradictory propositions] to be successively verified for one and the same thing, except (i) on account of the local motion of something, or (ii) on account of the passage of time, or (iii) on account of the production or destruction of some thing. (Book 1, distinction 30, question 4)

The realist had asserted this principle in a simple form, including only Ockham's clause (iii). But for Ockham, 'X is in motion' goes from being false to being true, not because X now acquires from its mover an accidental *thing*, <u>motion</u>, which before it lacked, but because through the passage of time it has come about that X, which was in one place, is sometime later in another.

Let us now place this theory into the larger scheme of things, that is, into the scheme of his grand nominalism. Overall, this is the structure of Ockham's remarkable argument that motion is unreal:

1. Ockham argues that the realist theory has a serious rational problem, because God could, using his absolute power,

destroy <u>motion</u> but preserve individual moving substances, and vice versa. Hence, the foremost convincing positive reason to posit <u>motion</u>, that it explains why things move, is eliminated.

2. Moreover, the second seemingly convincing positive reason to posit <u>motion</u> is that it explains how sentences of the form 'X is in motion' are sometimes true (or false). But Ockham takes this away as well, by giving his alternate semantics—connotative semantics—and offering the following subargument to explain the truth and falsity of sentences of this sort containing the word 'motion':

   (a) The principle of contradictories is not so simple. There are more ways for sentences to change truth-value besides things coming into being or going out of existence. The principle of contradictories must be 'opened up' to include two other possibilities, listed below as (i) and (ii):

   It is impossible for contradictories to be successively verified for one and the same thing, except (i) on account of the local motion of something, or (ii) on account of the passage of time, or (iii) on account of the production or destruction of some thing.

   (b) The term 'motion' is a connotative term, an abbreviation, signifying exactly what the following words in this nominal definition signify:

   X is in motion $=_{\mathrm{NDF}}$ X successively coexists in different places without intervening rest, continuously (Basically, X is here and at some other *time* it will be there [without intervening rest, continuously]).

   (c) Therefore, as is clear from this nominal definition, sentences like 'X is moving' are true or false depending on the passage of *time*, that is, the sentence 'X is moving' changes truth value due to clause (ii) above, not clause (iii), as the realists had said.

3. This subargument 2(a)–2(c) takes away the only other argument based on *reason* why we should posit <u>motion</u>.

4. Furthermore, neither *experience* nor *religious authority* require us to posit <u>motion</u> either. Not experience; we see moving things, certainly, but we do not see any accidental form <u>motion</u>. Again, the Bible directly mentions moving things, but it does not endorse Aristotelian theory of accidental forms such as <u>motion</u>; hence it is not religiously necessary to posit it.

5. By the razor, no extra-mental distinction among things should be assumed unless it can be proved by reason, or by unquestionable experience, or by some infallible religious authority. Hence, by 3 and 4 above, we ought not to posit <u>motion</u> at all.

CONCLUSION: Therefore, it is rational to say there is no such thing as <u>motion</u>, existing as a separate being in the world, in any way at all independent from moving things.

What Causes Local Motion?

Despite this amazing conclusion, Ockham does admit that things move by changing location; this is in fact how he defines motion. Given his reductive semantics, how does Ockham explain the causes of why things sometimes move locally? That is, even if he has told us which conditions make 'X is moving' true (it is here and at another time is there), he has not told us why things move. What makes things sometimes be here and at another time there?

Following Aristotle, Ockham says there are two kinds of local motion: that which begins from an *extrinsic cause*, and that which begins from an *intrinsic cause*. Beings that move from intrinsic causes are said to be *self-movers*. Without exception Ockham holds that self-movers move due to their essence, that is, due to their *fixed natures*. As we learned in Chapter 2, every being has an essence, and so a fixed nature determined by its essence, which makes it the kind of thing it is. Ockham believes in essences or natures in individuals; he just doesn't believe they are universal (as we saw in Chapter 4). The natures of self-movers explain their local motion; for example, the nature of earth is *the heaviest of the four elements*, and so anything made from earth always seeks the lowest point. So a stone moves down when dropped because it is composed mostly of earth, and so is heavier than the surrounding air, displacing it as its nature moves it to the lowest point. Similarly, a human being is an organic creature (an animal) who has a rational soul and a free will; this is its unchangeable nature. Since the animal part of us has capacities for nutrition, growth, and sensation, a human being can move locally for any of these reasons. But a human being also has a power for opposites, that is, a free will, and so can select objects presented to it by the intellect.

By contrast, local motions caused by extrinsic causes happen when one thing moves another. This idea is a little simpler generally, but there is also a big puzzle about a special kind of extrinsically caused local motion, called projectile motion, to be discussed shortly. Nevertheless, Ockham's basic picture of the mechanism of extrinsic local motion is simple: one thing moves another locally because the first thing is a solid body that smashes into the second thing, also a solid body.

Here, though, is the puzzle. Aristotle seems to have thought that, in cases of extrinsic causation, the mover must be kept in constant contact with the moved throughout the course of the motion. For example, an ox pulling a plow must be constantly yoked to the plow to move it. A classic example where this principle seems not to apply is projectile motion, say an arrow. An arrow leaves a bow with a certain velocity. The cause of its local motion is something extrinsic—namely, the moving bow-string. At the first instant of the motion the mover and the moved (cause and effect), are in contact with each other. But in any later instant of the motion this is not true; the contact is broken as the arrow flies through the air away from the bow. So too with all projectile motion. But if the cause of projectile motion is always (eventually) separated from the effect, how can it continue to serve as its cause? Or, to put it another way, how can there be causal action at a distance?

There seem to be two possible solutions to the difficulty: (1) posit something like inertia, or as the medievals called it, *impetus*, a property of the moving thing to stay in motion once put in motion, or (2) say that the cause really does somehow stay in contact with the effect. Modern people often (but not always) solve the problem as in (1) Aristotle thought that the only solution to the difficulty was (2) He developed his answer by positing a series of intermediate causes when the effect was at a distance. In the case of the arrow, he might say that the bowstring moves the arrow and the air behind the arrow, and that this air moves other air, and so on, with the arrow always out in front of this wave. This is much the way we understand sound today, for example; one part of the air near your mouth is made to move, and moves those parts next to them, which moves the parts next to them, etc. until the air near my ear is moved, which moves the tiny bones in my ear, etc. and I hear you speak. However, Ockham seems to have rejected both (1) and (2) and favored the idea that there can be causal action at a distance, and this fact can make Ockham seem modern, since, indeed, this is how we understand gravity and magnetism today. However, this part of Ockham's theory of motion is the least original. He did not have the notion of experimental science, and he was interested primarily in theology, after all.

Critique of Ockham's Theory of Motion

Although I will not presume to say whether Ockham or his realist opponents are correct about the status of motion, there are several interesting points to examine regarding the adequacy of Ockham's own definition of motion in particular, since many people find his definition quite reasonable. The most interesting point that can be made without definitively deciding the absolute correctness of either side is this: realist definitions of motion have one enormous advantage over Ockham's definition, namely, being able to account for the instantaneous truth of propositions about motion. Let me explain.

Ockham's account of motion, briefly recall, was that 'X is moving' means 'X is in a place at time t, and at $t^* \neq t$, X is (continuously, without rest) in another place'. Because it crucially involves the concept of the passage of time, Ockham's account of motion has the following odd property: the present tense statement 'X is moving', which seems for all the world to be true at any given instant of time in the interval of X's motion, is dependent for its truth on a state of affairs that transpires at a completely different time in that interval. But from this fact (which I will explain more fully with examples below), it can be shown that no sentence of the form 'X is moving at t' is determinately true at t, and present-tensed statements about motion must really be about the past or the future. In short, although it is somewhat counterintuitive, Ockham cannot hold that any statement of the form 'X is moving at t' is determinately true at t. The realist can easily assert that 'X is moving at t' is determinately true at t, as we will see in more detail at the end of this section, because for him 'X is moving at t' results from X having the accidental form <u>motion</u> at t. Thus, for the realist, the cause of the proposition's truth (the form) and the effect (the proposition's truth) are always simultaneous.

A thought experiment will help to make this point clearer, and also to reveal most sharply why this deficiency is a problem for the Ockhamist. Picture a pair of identical toy cars on a table-top. We have an overhead view looking down on the table. Imagine that one car is in the middle of the table, to one side, and that on the other side another car sits a few feet behind the first, facing the same direction. If we pushed the second car it would soon catch up to the first and eventually pass it, but for an instant, the two would be side-by-side in the middle of the table. Imagine further that we have a camera that takes instantaneous photographs. We take a snapshot of the initial situation just described, say at time t_1, with Car 1 sitting still, and Car 2 sitting still behind it. Figure 6.1 represents an instantaneous photograph taken at t_1:

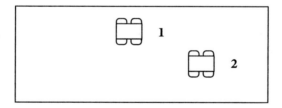

FIGURE 6.1

Both cars are at rest.

Now give Car 2 a light shove forward (Figure 6.2) . . .

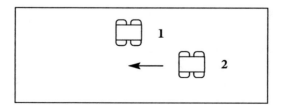

FIGURE 6.2

. . . and then, just at the instant it comes level with Car 1—call this instant t_2—we take another picture. Figure 6.3 represents a photograph taken at t_2:

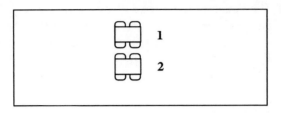

FIGURE 6.3

Next, we suppose that Car 2 keeps going, passing Car 1 entirely:

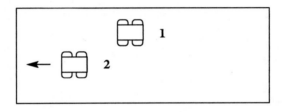

FIGURE 6.4

Finally, imagine that Car 2 comes to rest at a later time, say t_3, and at that moment we take a third photograph, represented in Figure 6.5:

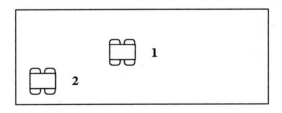

FIGURE 6.5

The entire interval of Car 2's motion we will call *i*:

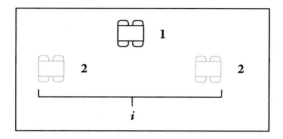

FIGURE 6.6

We now ask several questions about the resulting photographs, and in particular about Figure 6.3, when the cars were next to each other:

Q #1: Can we tell which car is moving merely by looking at the photograph of time t_2 in Figure 6.3?

A: Obviously, no. For all we can tell, either one could be moving, or they could both be at rest or both in motion.

Q #2: Is Car 2 truly a moving car at time t_2?

Be careful before you answer here, and make sure the question is clear to you. I'm not asking if Car 2 can move a certain distance *during* an instant, that is, during t_2, obviously it cannot; instants have no duration, and so in that sense nothing can cross a distance during an instant. What I am really asking is whether Car 2 is properly described at instant t_2 as a *moving thing*, or in other words, whether the sentence 'Car 2 is moving at t_2' is true at t_2.

A: *It depends on how you define motion.* If we use Ockham's definition, we *must* say 'no'. It takes some explanation to see why this is true and why it is a big problem.

First, notice that by Ockham's general definition, Car 2 has definitely moved, since in our example during interval *i* it successively coexisted in different places, without intervening rest, continuously. It was in one place at t_1, and successively, continuously, without resting, it was in a different place at t_3, where t_1 and t_3 are the distinct endpoints of interval i. (Remember, Car 2 did not stop at t_2, we just photographed it at the instant it came even with Car 1; the motion was truly continuous and without intervening rest.) But now let us focus on the instant we asked about above, t_2, and let us apply Ockham's definition to the particular instant at hand: According to Ockham's definition, is the sentence 'Car 2 is moving at t_2' true at t_2? Well, in order for it to be true at t_2, it would have to be the case that, at t_2, Car 2 successively coexisted in different places, without intervening rest, continuously. But this is impossible; nothing can coexist at different places at a single instant; hence by Ockham's definition, it cannot truly be said at t_2 that Car 2 is moving at t_2. For Ockham, the truth of 'Car 2 is moving at t_2' requires a certain state of affairs to happen at another instant of time outside t_2; hence the state of affairs that makes 'Car 2 is moving at t_2' true does not exist at t_2. Therefore, because a necessary condition for the truth of 'Car 2 is moving at t_2' is missing at t_2, 'Car 2 is moving at t_2' cannot be said to be true at t_2.

Or, again, we could explain the same point in terms of Ockham's expanded principle of contradictories. We said above that for Ockham, it is true that a thing moves if, during some passage of time, it is in one place and then another (continuously, without rest). But there is no passage of time at an instant; therefore for any instant t in the interval i, it cannot be true at t to say that 'Car 2 moving at t'. According to Ockham's theory of motion, a thing must exist in at least two distinct instants of time in order for it to be true that the thing is moving at any given time. And while this bare assertion at first seems correct and unproblematic, and is reasonable when explaining past tense sentences ('Car 2 *moved*' is true because it *was* there and is now here), when coupled with Ockham's general theory of motion this fact implies that *a present tense sentence such as 'X is moving at an instant' can never be true at that very instant.* We must answer 'no' to Q #2 according to Ockham's definition just as we answered 'no' to Q #1.

However (and here is the problem), this answer is totally counter-intuitive. It is evidently true that 'Car 2 is moving at t_2'; this is in fact the important difference between the two cars in the photograph in Figure 6.3. Indeed, the difference between the two cars at time t_2 is simply stated: Car 1 is at rest, hasn't been anywhere else in the recent past, and won't be anywhere different in the near future, while Car 2 previously got a push from us and will keep going. It seems, contrary to what Ockham's definition tells us, the correct answer to Q #2 is that Car 2 is a moving thing at t_2, and 'Car 2 is moving at t_2' is in fact true at t_2.

If you tend to think that Ockham is right, because nothing has velocity at an instant, be reminded that the entire edifice of modern physical science depends on the possibility of measuring velocity in an instant, because this is precisely the central idea of the calculus. In fact, calculus in some sense just *is* the assumption that one can calculate the instantaneous rate of change of one variable with respect to another (say time and distance), provided the change is smooth and continuous. In fact, if we had a mathematical function describing the motion of Car 2 in terms of time, we could, by first determining the derivative of this function and then using simple substitution and arithmetic, compute exactly what the velocity of Car 2 actually *is* at time t_2. But since by Ockham's definition 'Car 2 is moving at t_2' cannot even be true at t_2, if Ockham's definition of motion were correct, calculus, and hence all the sciences depending on it, including modern physics, would be nonsensical. After all, you can't measure the velocity of Car 2 at time t_2 if it is false at t_2 that Car 2 is a moving thing. How could a thing not moving have velocity?

Ockham has in effect conflated *what it means for a thing to move*, on the one hand, with *how we know a thing is moving* on the other. We know a thing is moving now by seeing if it is somewhere else a little bit in the future. But if in order to *be* moving a past or future state of affairs must also exist, it can never sensibly be said at the present instant that the thing is moving *now*. Just because we must wait and see to tell if a thing is moving does not mean that the reality of its moving is likewise determined by some past or future event. A thing in motion now is a moving thing right now, as the second instantaneous photograph of the two cars shows us: although looking at the photograph won't let us know which car is the moving car, nevertheless, one of the cars is *in reality* a moving thing at that instant, the other is not. The cars are metaphysically different in a way that Ockham can't account for.

Notice that the realist account, which posits a successive accident <u>motion</u>, will evade this same objection very easily, since, on that realist account 'X is moving at t' is true at instant t because an accident of <u>motion</u> inheres in X at t, or it is false at t because the accident does not inhere in X at *t*. The realist account, whatever its other defects, gives a perfectly clear account of what it means for present tense sentences about motion to be true at the present instant, and so has at least the virtue of not obviously conflicting with calculus. We may have here discovered a place where Ockham's famous one-two punch—connotation theory and the razor—gets rid of too much.

The Nature of Physics

Finally, let's consider: what does this committed nominalist think physics is about, if not <u>motion</u>? His answer is clear, and somewhat strange. You have to read it for yourself to believe it:

> First, we must take note that natural science, just as any other science, is about universals and concepts, not about things. (Davies's translation of Ockham in *Ockham on Aristotle's Physics*, p. 2)

Strange to say, Ockham holds that physics, like *all* sciences, is about universal concepts. A science is nothing more than a system of propositions in mental language. How in the world does he come to this position? To understand Ockham's motivation, it helps to consider the realist view for a moment. So imagine we are realists, and we want to object to Ockham's theory of motion as given above. We might argue like this:

> You say there is no <u>motion</u>, Ockham, only moving things; to be exact, you say there are only individual, singular moving things. Okay then, what is physics about? It can't be about individual singular moving things, because physics, like all sciences, is *universal* and *general*, not *singular* and *particular*. Physics is not about the motion of this planet or that planet, this rock or that rock, but of things in general, hence of the general, universal <u>motion</u>, just as biology is a science of the universal natures of various animals.

Now Ockham can't get out of this one, it seems, because Aristotle says clearly and unequivocally that "science is of the universal." But as we have seen, Ockham believes that the only thing in reality which is in any way universal is concepts, and they are only universal in the sense that they *apply to many things*. So Ockham seems trapped—if nothing outside the mind is universal, and science is universal, then science is not about anything outside the mind. But this doesn't seem right; some sciences may be about concepts—for example, logic, cognitive psychology, linguistics—but other sciences, which the medievals called *real sciences*, seem to be about extra-mental things—for example, biology is about frogs and trees (or their natures if we are realists), meteorology about wind and rain, (or their natures), and so on. How can we distinguish real sciences from the rest if all sciences are about concepts? Is Ockham really saying that meteorology is about wind$_m$, and not about wind itself, or the nature of wind?

Yes, he is. He accepts Aristotle's claim that science is of the universal, but he absolutely will not budge on his nominalism—nothing whatsoever outside the mind is in any way at all universal. It follows immediately that science is not about the world outside the mind.

Strange as this sounds, when you get down to it Ockham's views aren't so crazy. Really, he is just using the word 'science' in a fussy way. Science, Ockham says, is a form of knowledge, and knowledge exists in human minds, so it is a quality of knowing subjects. Hence a science, as an organized system of true propositions in the minds of knowing subjects, is really nothing more or less than a system of propositions in a mind. How do we distinguish one science from another? Well, different sciences have different subjects. "Aha," the realist says, believing he has the upper hand, "what could those different subjects be but the different extra-mental items the sciences study? Animal biology differs from botany in that the former studies frogs and frog natures while the latter studies trees and tree natures. But you don't believe sciences are about the outside world, so how can you distinguish them?" Ockham's reply is simple. The science of animal biology is a certain system of propositions in the mind of the animal biologist, for example, one including such propositions as:

Fish have vertebrae.

Dogs are mammals.

etc.

and likewise the science of botany is a certain system of propositions in the mind of the botanist, for example:

Magnolias are evergreens.

Ferns have sporangia.

etc.

What makes the two different is indeed their different subjects, but here we do not mean 'subjects' in the sense of 'the thing we are studying', but rather, 'subject' in the sense of 'the grammatical subjects of the propositions'. That is, the animal biologist and the botanist differ in that the propositions in their minds have different grammatical subjects:

Fish have vertebrae.	*Magnolias* are evergreens.
Dogs are mammals.	*Ferns* have sporangia.
etc.	etc.

The animal biologist has in his head, for example, the mental term fish$_m$ as the *subject* of the mental proposition 'Fish have vertebrae.' The botanist, insofar as she is a botanist, has the mental terms for plants in the propositions in her mind instead, e.g., magnolias$_m$.

Is Ockham saying that botany is about, for example, the mental word magnolias$_m$? Yes, he is. But is botany then a real science? Well, of course it is, because the term magnolias$_m$ in personal supposition stands for things outside the mind. Sciences like botany *deal with* extra-mental things like magnolia trees, yes. But magnolia trees are not the object of the science—the object is the propositions about magnolia trees; nor are magnolia trees the subject of the science—the subject is properly speaking the mental term magnolias$_m$, among others. So botany is 'about' real magnolia trees only in this crude and broad sense—because botany knowledge contains mental propositions whose subject term is, for example, magnolias$_m$.

Now this seems like a maddening dodge at first, but Ockham has a serious point in insisting on this. If he did not, then we could use Aristotle's claim that science is of the universal to try to force Ockham to admit that if there is a science of botany there must be, for example, extra-mental universals like <u>magnolia tree</u>. But this he will never do. His only other choice is to say that the universal the science of botany is about is the universal *term* magnolias$_m$, for example. This commits him to the existence of whatever the mental term magnolias$_m$ personally supposits for, of course, but remember, for Ockham magnolias$_m$ personally supposits for all the individual, concrete, extra-mental magnolia trees.

To return to physics: what would Ockham say physics is about? Directly, the objects of physics are the mental propositions physicists have in their heads insofar as they are physicists, for example, 'Local motion is successive change of place', or 'Motion at a distance is possible'. What is the subject of physics? Many things, but chiefly, motion$_m$, since this mental term appears as subject in many of the mental propositions in the heads of physicists, insofar as they are physicists.

To sum up, although the outlook here may seem strange, the deep motivation is his nominalism; because the only universal things he believes in are concepts in the mind, if science is of the universal, it follows that science must be first and foremost in the mind. In saying this he is not trying to be funny, or to claim that science is therefore subjective in our modern sense of the term, he is only trying at all costs to consistently preserve his insight that the only things that are real outside the mind are individual substances and their individual qualities, and that nothing outside the mind is in any way universal. In short, he is preserving, in the face of Aristotle's remarks on science, his firm commitment to radical nominalism.

We often associate nominalism with a certain scientific cast of mind. I hope this discussion has shown that a really thoroughgoing nominalism such as Ockham's has peculiarities and even outright difficulties dealing with elements of the modern attitude toward science.

A General Critique of Connotative Reduction

We have now seen connotative reduction used to collapse the categories (Chapter 4), and even to argue specifically against the existence of motion as a real, distinct thing outside the mind (Chapter 6, pp. 117–120). We also found some reason to be cautious about Ockham's reduction of motion in particular, having showed that it perhaps cuts away too much (pp. 122–28). But are there any *general* philosophical dangers associated with the use of connotation theory? Or can it be used any time we want reduce an entity in someone else's ontology?

Walter Chatton once said that if Ockham was right, and it was acceptable to try to use connotative reduction and the razor anywhere you wanted to break down other people's distinctions, then you could not stop the following argument, which concludes that God is the devil. Here is Chatton's argument, parodying Ockham's reductive methods:

> [Using only connotative reduction] there would be no way convincingly to show that God and the devil are not the same being – neither through sacred Scripture, nor through ecclesiastical determinations, nor through the words of the Saints. The reason is that, if it is in any way possible to show that God is not the devil, it would be through certain authorities saying resoundingly that 'God is not the devil'. But we could never prove that things are this way through the authorities themselves if connotative reduction is used without restraint, because we could just say, using connotation theory, that the name 'God' and the name 'devil' are names of one and the same entity [call it the 'God/devil'], and that nevertheless, the different names connote diverse things. We could say that the name 'God' connotes the God/devil as the cause of good effects, and the name 'devil' signifies the same God/devil as being the immediate partial cause of evil effects. And in this way you could still explain why it is true that one and the same thing is evil and good, simply on account of the fact that there are diverse *connotata* for the words 'God' and 'the devil'. (From Chatton's *Prologue*, question 2, article 1.)

Of course the Ockham-style argument here is absurd and its conclusion would have been blasphemous. But that is exactly the point. Ockham's connotative reduction can reduce any distinction just by telling a little story about terms. Ockham's general strategy of connotative reduction, with nothing else to balance it, is *too* reductive.

Chatton's point is perfectly general: it seems any inference of the form

(1) *a* does good;

(2) *b* does evil;

(3) therefore, *a* is not *b*,

or, more generally still:

(1) *a* has property *P*;

(2) *b* has not-*P*;

(3) therefore, *a* is not *b*,

could be blocked by connotation theory and the razor. For example, to block an argument of the first form, we could just claim that even though *a* is good and *b* is evil, nevertheless *a* is *b* (call the single entity in question '*a/b*'), because the name '*a*' connotes the good that *a/b* does while the name '*b*' connotes the evil that *a/b* does. If this kind of reasoning were generally acceptable, you could never argue for any distinction at all.

But more is true, says Chatton. If you could use connotative reduction without restraint, then any form of *predication* in which one thing is said of another would break down:

> If [connotative reduction] were always acceptable, human beings could have no certitude about any plurality of things, nor could we have certitude from the articles of faith, from the sacred Scripture, from Ecclesiastical determinations, or from the sayings of the Saints. The reason is that when they express the thought that *one thing is not another*, it could always be said, in the theological case as well as in the case of philosophy, that they say this only because *one thing* is connoted through the subject and *the other* is connoted through the predicate, and hence any proposition can be denied when it predicates *one thing* of *another*, [where these things are distinct]. (From Chatton's *Prologue*, question 2, article 1.)

Think about it this way: suppose we agree it is true that '*a* has property P', and we normally assume in such cases that *a* ≠ P, that is, that *a* and P are distinct. No matter what *a* and P are, Ockham could always say no, *a* and P aren't really distinct after all, in fact P's aren't *real* at all—the proposition '*a* is P' simply means that '*a* exists P-ly', that is, '*a* exists in a P way'. Ockham could destroy any ability to predicate one thing of another. This is just too much for Chatton. He says: "I prefer to posit more things than to give way to such concessions."

The conclusion of Chatton's objections is not that connotation theory is incorrect, but that (1) it cannot simply be assumed to be the correct analysis in any random case, since 1(a) application to every case would yield the impossibility of reasoning from authority, and 1(b) application to certain particular cases is just silly (the God/devil); and (2) connotative analysis would seem, all by itself, to reduce to absurdity by licensing the collapse of any distinction, and indeed of predication of distinct things.

This leads to the strange but unavoidable result that, in order to know whether or not Ockham's application of connotation theory is correct in any particular instance of a term T, we need to know, not that a connotative analysis of T *can be given*, but that connotative analysis in this case *is in fact correct* for T. In other words, we need to know that 'motion', 'cause', 'time', and so forth, are *in fact* connotative terms, not merely that they can be regarded as such. But Ockham never provides any arguments of this kind, and it is difficult to imagine how he could.

Ockham Asked to Explain Himself

Despite Ockham's efforts to clarify his views on the razor and God's absolute power, and to extend his views away from theologically dangerous subjects to more mundane ones such as physics, he found himself increasingly under fire. Although he worked intensely on many commentaries on Aristotle's physics throughout this period of 1321–1323, it was already too late. In 1323, he was summoned to a Franciscan provincial chapter in Cambridge, presumably by a superior in the Order, to explain himself further. Did he really mean to collapse the categories and to deny the existence of relations? Did he really mean to prune the tree of beings down to a mere stump, and a narrow stump at that? If so, what did that mean for the doctrine of the Trinity, and for God's relationship to the creation?

Moreover, brilliant as he was, he could not entirely confine himself to commentaries on physics during this period, as might have been wise. Just before he was summoned to Cambridge, Ockham took the time to summarize everything we have talked about so far, especially his metaphysical views, and disguise them as an introductory treatise on logic. The book wasn't merely a Trojan horse against the realists; it was also a genuine treatise on logic and semantic theory, and certainly in that book Ockham discussed many standard topics in Aristotelian-style logical theory of his time. But its opening chapters plainly contain the suggestion that his realist opponents were illogical, and, wanting to prevent them from leading any more Oxford students astray in metaphysics, he smugly titled his work *Summa logicae*, 'The Complete Book of Logic', then gave it a strong nominalist slant. The implication, of course, is that when one knows everything there is to know about logic, one is not a metaphysical realist.

Ockham was just completing this massive tome, consolidating his entire nominalist system, when the trouble we have seen looming ominously finally caught up with him at the highest levels. He had caught the attention of the Pope.

7

The Teacher Interrupted (1323–1328)

OCKHAM'S SHOWDOWN WITH THE POPE

In order for the formal proceedings against Ockham to go as far as they did, it seems he must have first caught the attention of a powerful person nearer to him; why else should the Pope bother with an obscure English friar?

Some scholars suspect that Oxford Chancellor John Lutterell went directly to Pope John XXII in 1323 with several dozen theses which Ockham had maintained and which needed examination for heretical content. Other scholars blame fellow Oxonian John of Reading, regent master of the Franciscans at Oxford in 1320–21, for bringing Ockham to the attention of papal authority in 1322. In a move that foreshadowed his summons to Avignon, the spring of 1323 found William in Cambridge, at a Franciscan provincial chapter, 'clarifying' certain worrisome claims he had recently been defending, including especially his claims to have reduced the ten categories of being, as discussed in Chapter 4.

Whoever was responsible for bringing Ockham to the attention of the Pope, the desired effect was achieved. The Pope himself convened a committee to determine if Ockham was teaching heresy at Oxford, and Ockham was required to go to Avignon (in modern France) to answer the charges and explain himself in person. Most of the members of this examining committee—in fact, all of them save one—were metaphysical realists.

He left England in May 1324. We don't know exactly how long the journey took, and Channel crossings were still somewhat dependent on weather conditions, but it seems he arrived no later than the summer of that year. Again, we don't know exactly how he spent his time there, which amounted in the end to four years.

However, we must not imagine him jailed or in a witness box during this time, like a defendant in a modern secular criminal trial. Indeed, there is little reason to suppose that the examination of his works would have taken very much of *his* time at all. There is some evidence that he passed the days editing one of his last philosophical works, the *Quodlibets*, which, as mentioned in the previous chapter, represents seven debates Ockham participated in. Parts 6 and 7 of the *Quodlibets* may even have been argued and written in Avignon. On the other hand, neither should we imagine him living in luxurious apartments in the Palace of the Popes with no responsibilities at all. The sumptuous and extraordinarily well-fortified *Palais des Papes* (still standing in Avignon today) did not exist in 1324; Ockham was housed in the older, less grand residence which it replaced. Moreover, he would still have been at the command of Franciscan superiors. As we will soon learn, this last fact was pivotal to everything that happened next.

We have already seen in Chapter 5 how his metaphysics raised some eyebrows. However, it turns out that not only his innovative arguments on language and ontology, but also some of his ideas in epistemology and ethics elicited reactions. It is almost as though he was incapable of responding to the hostility around him by toning down his approach in other areas; he pushed on with his usual energy despite the external threat to him. In this chapter I will outline some of the more controversial aspects of his ideas on epistemology and ethics, even though doing so will sometimes take us back to Aristotle and to Ockham's earlier writings. Given the point we have reached in his story, this is our last chance to complete our picture of his non-political philosophy; after the situation with John XXII came to a crisis in 1328, he only wrote political philosophy.

Philosophy of Mind and Action in the Middle Ages

Although their novelty is sometimes overstated in the secondary literature, Ockham really did seem to hold some strange and interesting views in epistemology and ethics. In order to discuss these views, a reorientation may first be necessary for the modern reader. Although to us the philosophy of knowledge and the philosophy of right and wrong might seem dissimilar disciplines (even if certain connections between them are admitted) in the medieval conception of things these two areas had a great deal in common. A *person*, in this period, is a being with both intellect and will, and these aspects of mind are, respectively, the bases for epistemology and ethics. In a sense both disciplines fall under a kind of pragmatic philosophy of action together with a frankly mechanistic philosophy of mind.

Here is another way to think about the naturalness of this pairing. In the Middle Ages, ethics was a theory of certain operations of *anima*, equally well translated as 'soul' or as 'mind'; in particular, it was a theory of those operations of intellect and will leading to good moral acts and producing good moral habits. And again, epistemology was a theory of *anima*; in particular it was a theory of those operations of intellect and will leading to good epistemic outcomes in our acts of knowledge, belief, and faith, and (strange though it may sound to us to speak of habits in this context), the habits of knowledge, belief, and faith that went with such acts.

Aristotle's Basic Picture of Intellection and Some Problems with It

According to Aristotle, *cognition* or *understanding* is the chief power of the human soul, and all cognition begins with *sensation*. Indeed, he divides cognition into two kinds, *sensory* and *intellective*: in the first we see, hear, or touch particular sensory objects; in the second we understand their universal natures.

Aristotle's theory of soul is famously difficult. For present purposes we will skate over the difficulties and simply present a medieval-Aristotelian view of the operations of the intellect. The view I end up describing may not have been held in *exactly* this form by anyone in the Middle Ages, but its outlines do fit what was generally held, and it will give us sufficient background to begin to understand Ockham's theory of knowledge.

SENSORY PART

Objects in the world of sense have structures which can be sensed and understood, called 'forms'. These we have discussed before. Sensory objects naturally transmit packets of sensible (= able to be sensed) information about their sensible, accidental forms; some thinkers focus on the mechanics of this transmission, postulating that they enter a medium, like the air, before reaching the eyes, ears, or other organs of perception, of a sensing animal. Others pass over these details of transmission. Howsoever the forms of objects actually reach us, everyone agrees that they are picked up by the appropriate sense organs of animals, which organs are naturally equipped to receive such information—the ears pick up sound-forms, the eyes pick up sight-forms, and so on. These sense organs are literally stamped with this information (= the forms) as warm wax is stamped by a seal-ring. The resulting impression is the form of the object about to be sensed, and is called a 'sensible species'. So far the process operates below the conscious level.

Next, the stamping of the sense organs stimulates a further power, called the 'sense-faculty', which assembles these received species into a new mental object called a 'fantasm', which is something like a simulation or representation of the individual object being sensed. At this stage the person sensing the object is aware of sensation taking place. Finally, the fantasm is stored in a mental faculty called in Latin *fantasia*, or in English 'the imaginative faculty'. Overall, we see here an underlying pattern of a five-stage process: we have (1) an input (forms from a sensible object); (2) a reception (in a sense organ); (3) a production (of a sensible species); and (4) a final product (a fantasm), which is (5) stored (in the fantasia).

Intellective Part

While all animals have sensation, only human beings have an intellective function to their *anima*. As regards the structure of human intellection, Aristotle insisted that, as it is with sensation, so it is with intellection. In practice this means that each element of the five-part sensory process we just saw must have a counterpart in the process of intellection. So, to keep the two stories parallel, we need five things to happen in the intellect: an input, a reception, a production, and a final product, which is stored somewhere.

The easy parts to explain are the input and the final product. Clearly the input for the intellectual process is the final product of the sensory process, that is, the fantasm. Moreover, the final product of this intellectual process is a universal concept of the object originally sensed. Thus the beginning and end of intellection are clear. The details of the middle bits vary depending on how one reads Aristotle, but many people in the Middle Ages agreed that the fantasm is taken up or received by another part of the mind, which reception is called an *intelligible species*; this stage seems merely to consist of the intellective soul being informed or impressed by the fantasm. Once in this state, the intelligible species' particularizing features are stripped away or *abstracted* by something called the *active intellect*, leaving the final, perfectly general product of intellection, a universal concept of the thing understood. This concept is then stored in memory and can be retrieved for the purpose of thinking.

Let's imagine a concrete example that we can refer back to throughout this discussion. Suppose that I am on a walk and I stop to regard a particular tree, say, Maggie Magnolia. Like any sensible object, Maggie constantly emanates sensible forms from her, which are, by some process or other, delivered to my eyes. Because my eyes function correctly, and are of the right sort to receive visual information, they are stamped with visual forms from Maggie: her shape, leaf-color, and so forth. Similarly for other sense modalities. All this information, stamped on my organs, assembles into a sensible species of Maggie, from which my sense faculty produces an image, or fantasm, which is stored in the fantasia. Notice, although a usable image of Maggie now exists, we should not yet say that I am thinking about her, or cognizing her, because my intellect has not yet become involved. Although a lot has happened, we should think of the activity so far as nearly instantaneous, automatic, and mostly unconscious; as of yet I do not identify her as a tree.

In the stage of intellection my intellective soul takes over the fantasm of Maggie from the fantasia, and it is somehow impressed into my mind, although not consciously, in a manner analogous to the reception of sensory forms from the external object in the process of sensation. This impression of the fantasm is an intelligible species of Maggie, and it is in suitable condition for my active intellect next to strip away whatever is particular in this impression—the cast of the sun on her leaves, the squirrel in her lower braches, the lovers' initials carved in her trunk—none of these things is properly speaking part of any concept of *a tree*, whether of general accidental qualities such as her color, or of substantial features such as her species and genus. By setting these particularities aside, my mind has abstracted a universal concept, which allows me to think generally of trees. This part of the process is conscious; I now actively think of Maggie as a tree. With the concept stored in memory I am able to think about trees again at a later time.

We can summarize the discussion by putting these two processes together into a ten-part schema of cognition. The first five stages are sensory, the last five intellective; I have put the names of the active powers in this process in boldface type, and the products of their activities in italics:

> (1) a **sensible object** transmits its sensible forms to a human being, which forms (2) strike the **sense organs**, producing a *sensible species* which (3) stimulates the **sense faculty** to produce (4) a *fantasm* which (5) is stored in the **fantasia**; then (6) the **fantasia** sends out the stored *fantasm*, which (7) strikes **some passive intellectual power** which receives it, producing an *intelligible species* which (8) stimulates **the active intellect** to abstract from it (9) a *concept* which (10) is stored in the **memory**.

This account has three very odd features that worried Ockham, and led him to modify it in interesting ways. I discuss two of these features next, and a third a little later.

Problem #1

The first problem that bothered Ockham is the sheer clutter of this account. Indeed, any nominalist might well balk at the complicated mental ontology necessary to make this account run, and Ockham was a nominalist's nominalist. Some elements of the explanation are quite innocuous; nearly everyone believes in the existence of sensible objects and concepts. But this account adds more: fantasms, the fantasia, two flavors of intellect (active and passive), as well as the intelligible species (what is this thing, really?). Ockham preferred a sparser picture of the mind, and would rather postulate fewer things if possible, on account of the razor. Moreover, for a nominalist like Ockham, who only allowed those entities which seemed absolutely necessary by reason, religion, or experience, it was not enough that many people believed in the real existence of concepts; he would assume nothing about the ontological status of concepts without his own investigation. So, what are concepts? For them to fit with Ockham's 'Stump of Beings' from Chapter 4, it seems they could only be individual substances or individual qualities. If substances, what sort of existence could they have? Are universal concepts in any way universal in existence?

Problem #2

The second problem is that it seems this account partitions the human mind according to such a strict duality that experience of individuals is associated exclusively with sensation, while general knowledge is associated with intellection. But this raises a difficulty: it makes it hard to see how there are any particular intellectual concepts at all. For if sensation is of the individual and intellection is of the universal, then how can I have a concept of this individual, say, a concept of Maggie Magnolia? Surely I do have a concept proper to her, which I use when I think only of her. But if intellection always abstracts, then how could any particularity survive the abstractive process, and so how could any particularity exist in any concept at all? Problem #2 need not have bothered realists as much, since they believe that individuals and universals both exist in the world; hence they have an easy way of talking about how we might form both individual and universal concepts. But a nominalist as strict as Ockham does not have recourse to such an expedient. He must explain the universality of concepts by an entirely different means.

Ockham's Basic Outlook on Cognition: The *Fictum* Theory and the *Intellectio* Theory

In his student days these problems gave him quite a bit of trouble. His early view was that concepts were individual substances of a sort, that is, that they were beings of a certain sort, with relatively independent existence. What kind of existence? Obviously, as part of the immaterial soul they cannot be material, sensible Aristotelian *subjects* (in the sense of 'substrate' from Chapter 6). Rather, he decided, they had a different kind of existence, a kind of existence unique to objects of thought. Ockham expressed this point in his early theory of concepts by saying that concepts do not have *subjective reality* (Latin *esse subjectivum*) but rather have *objective reality* (Latin *esse objectivum*): the main thing about a concept is that some mind thinks it. Notice that this use of the term 'objective' has absolutely nothing to do with its modern use to denote something that is independent of the mind; here the meaning is exactly the opposite, in fact. The mind somehow has the power to fashion entities which have this objective reality, so we might also say that concepts are *ficta* (from Latin *fictum* = something fashioned). Thus Ockham's first theory of concepts states that they are *ficta*—not fictional or false, but fashioned by the mind – and that they have a unique kind of reality, which we could call 'object reality'. He did not come up with these distinctions on his own. Rather, he seems to have taken them over (with some modification or even distortion) from fellow Franciscan Peter Auriol (d. 1322), who studied in Paris, and, interestingly, had rather friendly relations with John XXII.

Now, if you are thinking that this so-called *fictum* theory of Ockham's doesn't sound like the work of a hard-headed nominalist and empiricist, you're right. Even if the *fictum* theory addresses some aspects of the two problems mentioned above, it does so clumsily, and doesn't clear away the clutter of the Aristotelian account either. Moreover, the *fictum* becomes a kind of intermediary between the mind and the thing it thinks about, thus compromising Ockham's basic intuition that we are directly aware of individual substances in the external world. Some of Ockham's contemporaries, Walter Chatton in particular, noticed that Ockham's early view made an ill fit with his metaphysics and epistemology, and that it violated the razor as well. The *fictum* theory didn't seem to make Ockham himself very happy either, and he quickly began casting around for an alternative.

Ironically, Chatton, the metaphysical realist, seems to have provided Ockham with the alternative view he was seeking. Ockham wanted a theory according to which concepts could be real beings, not merely fictive beings with objective reality, and he wanted them to be philosophically required by his rule of rational positing (Chapter 5). Remember, for Ockham, a real thing can only be an individual substance or an individual quality. Ockham had tried making concepts substances of a strange sort, but with mixed results. Why not think of concepts as qualities instead? In particular, Chatton suggested that we think of concepts as *qualities of the mind*. Thus, if my mind is thinking about trees, it is in a certain state—that is, it has a certain quality, thinking-about-trees—and this quality can be understood simply as the mental act of thinking (Latin *intellectio*) about the trees themselves. This so-called *intel-*

lectio theory, according to which my concept of X is just my act of thinking about X's, solved many, many problems for Ockham.

First, it gets rid of a needless intermediary between mind and world; second, it accords more with the razor. And in short, it solves Problem #1 above. Third, it does all this without leaving any temptation to posit universals essences as the real-world counterparts of universal concepts. In Ockham's *intellectio* theory, taken over from Chatton, my concept or mental term tree$_m$ is not caused by nor linked with a universal essence tree, but is just an individual quality of my mind; it is just my act of thinking of individual trees in a certain way, that is, according to their specific resemblance, no one tree more than any other. Thus, a universal concept as an *intellectio* is easy to understand, and is metaphysically acceptable to Ockham's nominalism; the account refers only to an individual substance (my mind) and an individual quality of it (my mental act of thinking of trees), plus the individual substances I am thinking about (the trees themselves). Fourthly and finally, in answer to Problem #2 above, this account is easily extended to particular concepts as well; just as my concept of tree is my act of thinking about them, my concept of Maggie Magnolia, a particular tree, is simply my mental act of thinking about *her*.

Despite all these advantages, Ockham was somewhat hesitant to adopt the theory at first, possibly in part because it was being advanced by a relentless critic. Nevertheless, by the time he reached the period of life we are investigating here, he had rejected the *fictum* theory completely and fully adopted the *intellectio* theory instead.

Intuitive and Abstractive Cognition

In addition to the two problems discussed above, there is yet a third problem, the solution of which led Ockham to further innovations.

Problem #3

On the Aristotelian account, if I saw a particular tree, say Maggie Magnolia, and formed a concept from her, I would of course retain the fantasm from this experience, and so at any later time, whether Maggie is around or not, I could go through steps 6–10 again, and extract a new concept from my fantasm of her. In short, I could think about her later without her being around; perhaps I saw her outside yesterday and formed a concept, but now today behind the walls of my windowless study I could call up her fantasm again from the fantasia, extract a concept, and think of her again. Notice these are two specifically distinct cognitive acts; the first we would tend to call 'perception', the second 'memory' or 'imagination'. But on the Aristotelian account of cognition above, these two specifically different acts have the same mechanical structure from steps 6–10 inclusive; they differ only in steps 1–5. However, notice that steps 1–5 are all arguably unconscious or preconscious. Hence, it seems we should conclude that *as far as I can tell, there is no detectable difference between thinking of a tree while I stand open-eyed in front of it, and thinking of that same tree when it is completely out of my sight.* But this is plainly wrong. There is an enormous difference in feel between the two acts of the mind, the first has the feeling of direct perception, the second of memory.

Ockham wanted a theory that would solve Problem #3 by explaining this difference, and yet would keep all of the advantages we have so far found in the *intellectio* theory of concepts. Ideally, such a theory would keep the ontology trim and would explain the origin of universal concepts, but without resorting to metaphysical realism about universals. To accomplish these ends, he invoked and then reworked a pair of ideas that had been around since Scotus, that of *intuitive cognition* versus *abstractive cognition*.

In Ockham's philosophy, intuitive cognition is like direct perception, while abstractive cognition is a bit like memory or imagination. Moreover, rather than simply associating sense perception with the singular and intellection with the general, Ockham regarded intuitive cognition of singulars as not only possible, but even common. This claim was based on an important fourfold distinction which results from subdividing these two kinds of cognition; we have: 1(a) intuitive sensory cognition and 1(b) intuitive intellective cognition, as well as 2(a) abstractive sensory cognition and 2(b) abstractive intellective cognition.

For Ockham, our direct encounters with individual objects currently present to us are *intuitive cognitions*. This kind of cognition subdivides. 1(a): If we merely perceive the object as such, without thinking about what it is or that it exists, in short, if we merely see it without going on to form thoughts about it, then this episode is called *intuitive sensory cognition*. 1(b): If, on the other hand, we have a direct encounter with an object present to us by intuitive sensation, and then, more than simply perceiving the object as such, we go on to form thoughts about what it now is or that it now exists, then this episode involves thinking, and so goes beyond intuitive sensory cognition; we should call this *intuitive intellectual cognition*. In short, for Ockham, the senses receive forms directly from a particular object in intuitive sensation, which experience can then cause an individual intuitive cognition of that particular.

Notice that this distinction is consistent with the way we solved Problem #2 above—the problem of how we can have concepts of particular individuals. According to Ockham's *intellectio* theory, a concept is general if it is the act of thinking about many things, or is particular if it is the act of thinking about one thing, and according to the distinction between 1(a) and 1(b), the ultimate source of our thoughts about particulars is our sensations of particulars. But since we can sense one thing or many things as easily as we can think about one thing or many things, the distinction between 1(a) and 1(b) in no way forces us to associate sensation uniquely with the particular and intellection uniquely with the universal. Problem #2 is now fully solved, and without recourse to a distinction between particular versus universal realities.

On the other side of the spectrum, when we consider things without their being present to our mind and senses, this is *abstractive cognition*. This kind of cognition also subdivides. (2a): If we merely remember the appearance of an object as it came to us in intuitive sensory cognition, without forming any thoughts about it, in short, if we remember it in recordative memory without going on to think about it, then this episode could be called *abstractive sensory cognition* (although Ockham used different terminology here). 2(b): If, on the other hand, we remember an object conceptually, and, more than simply recalling the appearance of the object as such, we form thoughts about what it is or that it existed (past tense), then this episode involves thinking, and so goes beyond abstractive sensory cognition; we could call this *abstractive intellectual cognition*.

The distinction between 1(a) and 1(b) was important to Ockham, as was the difference between 1 and 2—between intuitive cognition generally and abstractive cognition generally. However, he didn't really have a developed theory of 2(a). For these reasons, usually Ockham just used the phrase *abstractive cognition* when he talked about 2(b), in other words, he used the phrase 'abstractive cognition' when talking about abstractive intellectual cognition in particular, and I will also use the term 'abstractive cognition' in this way below.

Ockham had a very interesting way of explaining the difference between intuitive and abstractive cognition generally, one that allows us to answer Problem #3. The difference between abstractive and intuitive cognitions lies, not so much in what causes them, but rather in the kinds of effects they themselves are capable of causing.

Suppose one morning I am thinking of Maggie Magnolia as I stand looking at her directly. Then, later in the afternoon, suppose I think of her again in my study far away from where she grows. On both occasions, each of these intellective cognitions, abstractive and intuitive, will allow me to form the present-tense mental sentence:

1. 'Maggie Magnolia is a tree.'

And, more importantly, each of these acts of cognition can naturally *cause me to assent*, certainly, objectively, and involuntarily to mental sentence 1. For whether I am in front of her or back at home—whether, to put it technically, she is immediately causing an intuitive sensory cognition which leads me to an intuitive intellective cognition of her, or if instead I take an old memory image produced by a previous intuitive sensory cognition and form mental sentence 1 in her absence, thinking about her in my study using abstractive cognition—either type of cognition will cause me to judge 1 to be true. It only takes one actual look, one intuitive sensory cognition, for me to see that she is a tree, and once I do I always have enough information to be caused to agree afterward to this necessarily true proposition, whether I think about proposition 1 in front of her (by intuitive intellective cognition) or instead at home (by abstractive cognition). As Ockham puts it, both abstractive and intuitive cognition can cause my "evident assent" to a necessary proposition such as 'Maggie Magnolia is a tree.'

However, if I am merely remembering in my study (abstractive cognition), I will not give immediate, certain, and objective agreement to the mental sentence

2. 'Maggie Magnolia is in bloom.'

No merely abstractive cognition of a thing can give me certainty about a statement of this sort. Present tense, contingent propositions like 2 cannot be evidently assented to except by intuitive intellectual cognition; the blossoms of morning can drop by afternoon, hence memory is not enough for proposition 2. I must refresh the image by intuitive sensory cognition in order to be sure. Similarly, if more dramatically, the proposition stating her contingent existence

3. 'Maggie Magnolia is.'

will be assented to only by the power of an intuitive intellectual cognition, not by an abstractive one.

Can God Fool Us?

Looking carefully at proposition 3 immediately above, and thinking about intuitive and abstractive cognition, we might be tempted to say this: according to Ockham, intuitive cognition always causes me to make correct existential judgments, but abstractive cognition does not. After all, abstractive cognition can be 'fooled', in a sense. If I give assent to 'Maggie Magnolia is' by abstractive cognition while sitting in my study, it will not be an evident assent (that is, it will not be a certain, objective, and involuntary assent). Such an assent could only be given voluntarily and willfully by me, because it goes beyond any abstractive cognition; by itself a *memory* of Maggie is not enough to cause evident assent to a claim that she (currently) is. It might be wishful thinking. After all, perhaps Maggie was, and now, alas, she is not.

But intuitive cognition seems different; when, in her presence, I face the sentence 'Maggie Magnolia is', I will be caused by intuitive cognition to make an evident assent to it. And, it seems, if I go back the next morning after my original encounter with Maggie and, sadly, see that she is dug up and cut to pieces, then *that* intuitive cognition will cause my evident assent to the opposite proposition 'Maggie Magnolia is not'. So intuitive cognitions cause me to judge evidently that a thing is exists if it does, and that it does not exist if indeed it does not. In fact Ockham said *exactly* this about intuitive cognition in his commentary on the *Sentences*:

> An intuitive cognition of a thing is the sort of cognition in virtue of which it can be known whether a thing is or is not, so that if a thing is, immediately the intellect judges the thing to be and evidently knows that it is. . . . However, an abstractive cognition is one in virtue of which it cannot be evidently known of a contingent thing whether it exists or not. (*Sent.* I, Prologue I)

This sounds as though intuitive cognitions are reliable, or even infallible, and that abstractive cognitions are fallible, or even deceptive.

But this interpretation is a mistake. Ockham never did intend such a strange doctrine. After all, this view immediately raises the question: Can't God fool me about my intuitive cognitions? Surely, an omnipotent God can make me have an evident assent to a sentence like 'Maggie Magnolia is in bloom' or even 'Maggie Magnolia is', without Maggie really being present, or existing at all. In fact, Chatton himself asked Ockham this very question to see how far he would go in his theory of intuitive cognition—to get him to say just whether he thought it was infallible or not— thereby setting Ockham on the defensive about divine power at a time in his life when he could ill afford it.

Chatton objected that, on Ockham's view, if once an intuitive cognition has occurred, the correct judgment that the thing exists or not is an inevitable outcome. But suppose God wanted to trick me about what I am thinking by causing me wrongly to assent to the sentence 'Maggie Magnolia is', although Maggie has sadly been chopped down. According to Ockham, Chatton continues, there are two kinds of thinking, intuitive and abstractive, so God must pick a mode to deceive me in. He can't deceive me into false assent using abstractive cognition, because abstractive cognition cannot cause assent to contingent sentences like 'Maggie Magnolia is', as we saw above. But neither can God deceive me using an intuitive cognition, for, as Ockham says, intuitive cognitions cause me to judge evidently that a thing does not exist *if it does not exist*. By hypothesis Maggie does not exist, so any intuitive cognition he gave me will cause me to judge rather that she does not exist and assent instead to 'Maggie Magnolia is not'. Hence, I cannot be deceived by intuitive cognition either. But then, Chatton reasoned, if Ockham were correct, in no case can God deceive me about non-existent Maggie, and make me agree that she is when in fact she is not. So in general it seems that, according to Ockham, God cannot use my thinking to cause me to judge other than the facts.

Chatton wasn't getting this criticism from nowhere. Ockham really opened himself up to the misunderstanding that intuitive cognition is infallible by making the following seemingly incredible claim about intuitive cognition, again in his commentary on the *Sentences*:

> . . . if a completed cognition of this sort (i.e., intuitive), of something not currently existing, were to be preserved through divine power, by the power of this simple cognition the intellect would evidently cognize that the thing did not exist. (*Sent.* I, Prologue I)

Even if God makes me see Maggie existing by intuitive cognition, then preserves that cognition of Maggie existing but destroys Maggie herself, so that she is not, by intuitive cognition I will correctly judge that she is not. This makes it sound for all the world as though God cannot trick our intuitive cognition at all.

Faced with Chatton's objection to his theory of intuitive cognition, Ockham later clarified the theory, and, in this period just before Avignon (around 1323–24), he showed clearly he did not believe intuitive cognitions to be infallible. He responded to Chatton's objection in this way. Since an act of cognition is really distinct from an act of assent, God can cause the one and not the other. So, imagine as above that God wanted to trick me about what I am thinking by causing me wrongly to assent to the sentence 'Maggie Magnolia is', although he has obliterated Maggie. He can in fact trick me in this way, but it takes three miracles (interventions in the natural order) to pull it off. (1) First, God could directly cause an intuitive cognition of Maggie, existent, but (2) before this cognition causes me to judge correctly that she does exist, as it normally would, he could miraculously stop its effect, and then (3) cause me directly to have the (incorrect) judgment that Maggie does not exist. Or, similarly the other way: (1) First, God could directly cause an intuitive cognition of Maggie, non-existent (a view of her, chopped down, say), but (2) before this cognition causes me to judge correctly that she does not exist, as it normally would, he could miraculously stop its effect, and then (3) cause me directly to have the (incorrect) judgment that Maggie exists.

And in general, God can suspend the action of any (normally reliable) intuitive cognition, and then cause my false existential judgment *directly*. For example, if God first causes an intuitive cognition, then suspends its natural effect, then causes directly my assent to the (false) proposition 'Maggie Magnolia is', it seems he will have in effect tricked me, by using my own thinking to cause me to judge other than the facts.

All this business, which at first seems like much ado about nothing, can be explained as a rehash of the very seminal issue of God's absolute versus ordained power, as we saw in Chapter 5. As God actually made the world according to ordained power, intuitive cognitions are reliable. But he can, with his absolute power, intervene in the created order in the way described and bring deception and error out of even an intuitive cognition.

Is Ockham's response to Chatton adequate? It does not seem so, for on Ockham's elaborate imagining there is no real sense in which God has caused *me* to make a judgment at all. Indeed, it is not clear what the phrase 'God directly causes me to judge something' could even mean. There is a difference between 'God causing a judgment to exist in me' and 'me making a judgment'. To the extent that God is causing the judgment, it is no important sense *my judgment* any longer (except perhaps in the reduced sense of being an event that occurs in *my* head.) Chatton often made this kind of point against Ockham, and in fact Ockham seemed often to claim for God the ability to produce effects by absolute power without consideration for the causal origin of those effects.

Aristotle's Basic Picture of Ethics: Eudaimonism

Aristotle's ideas of the human good in his *Nicomachean Ethics* were terribly influential in the Middle Ages, and rightly so, for he presented a systematic and sober account of virtue, vice, character, and the good life which served medieval Latin philosophers admirably as a foundational schema for Christian theological additions. He argues that the highest good for a human being is that at which all human actions and crafts aim, but which aims at nothing outside itself; that is, the highest good is the most complete good. For humans this highest, most complete good is *eudaimonia*, which he defines as activity of the soul, over a long period, in accord with complete virtue. In short, freely to regulate one's own life firmly in accord with complete virtue over the long term is to flourish as a human being, to live well. *Eudaimonia*, sometimes translated 'happiness', nevertheless is not a merely state of well-being or a nice feeling. It is a certain kind of *activity*, in particular, the excellent exercise of our uniquely human powers—the virtues.

Hence virtue is a form of power; a kind of self-mastery. More specifically we can say Aristotle's theory of virtue has three parts:

1. Virtue is *excellence at characteristic function*, and so is tied to the kind of thing a human being is. A human being is essentially a rational thing.

2. A virtue is a *habit in the soul* (in conformity with reason), and so is acquired (or not) by training.

3. Each individual virtue is a *golden mean*; that is, a middle path between two vices, one of excess, one of deficiency. For example, when a person finds he needs to act in the face of fear, then we call *courage* that middle path between the extreme vices of *cowardice* on the one hand and *rashness* on the other.

In addition to courage, there are many other virtues which fit this pattern. For example, with regard to reacting to pleasure and pain, the virtue of *temperance* is the mean between insensibility and intemperance. With regard to managing anger, the virtue of *mildness* is the mean between irascibility and meekness. Aristotle discusses many others, such as honesty, magnanimity, appropriate shame, proper indignation, and friendliness.

Similarly and conversely, we have a theory of vice:

1. Vice is *poor performance at characteristic function*, and so is tied to the kind of thing a human being is. A human being is essentially a rational thing, so vice is irrational behavior of a certain kind.

2. A vice is a *habit in the soul*, (not in conformity with reason), and so is acquired (or not) by training.

3. Most individual vices lie on an extreme flanking a *golden mean*; that is, an extreme at the wing of a middle path. (Some vices, such as murder and adultery, do not fit this pattern, but are simply absolutely wrong.)

The sum total of a person's virtues and vices we might call that person's *character*.

Pragmatist that he is, Aristotle recognizes that full *eudaimonia* depends not only on virtue and effort, but also in some measure on luck, since action itself depends on luck. For example, if I am, simply by nature, the kind of person who faints at the sight of blood, then this physiological response will surely make it difficult for me to be courageous in saving the life of someone bleeding to death, not because I am a coward, but because, unfortunately, that virtue will be subject to 'external' interference due to my sensitivity. In this way, if I am otherwise courageous, bad luck can prevent my acting virtuously on a given occasion. Similarly and more generally, people with strong sex drives will struggle with chastity, poor people may have difficulty developing magnanimity or generosity; none of it on account of internal, willful, moral failings, but simply on account of the dumb luck of being as fortune made them. Today philosophers discuss such cases under the phrase 'moral luck'. We will come back to this issue shortly, because Ockham had strong views about it.

Finally, Aristotle held that the various virtues are united by their reliance on the practical intellect—on *prudence* or *wisdom*—and so have a kind of unity. In developing prudence, we develop our capacity for virtue generally. Some virtues are necessarily connected, such as courage and honesty.

Mediaeval Christian Reactions to Aristotle

The *Nicomachean Ethics* was an extremely well-respected book in the Latin world throughout the later Middle Ages. There were some things in the *Ethics* almost everybody agreed with, and some things almost everybody disagreed with, and some things they all fought with each other about.

AGREEMENT WITH ARISTOTLE

1. Most agreed to the basic framework, especially to *habit*, *rationality*, and the *practical intellect* (*=prudence*) interacting with the *will*.

2. The notion of habit and virtue was applied to religion to explain the *theological virtues* mentioned by Paul in 1 Corinthians 13: faith, hope, and charity. However, they also still accepted the existence of Aristotle's original list of moral virtues.

3. The idea of the golden mean, and Aristotle's list of moral virtues was deemed acceptable.

DISAGREEMENT WITH ARISTOTLE

1. No Christian could agree that the ultimate goal of human existence was *eudaimonia* during earthly life. Mediaeval theologians followed Augustine in holding that heaven is the ultimate human good.

2. Similarly, they could not agree to the possibility of reaching the highest good substantially by our own efforts, without divine help. For Aristotle all you need is the hard work of virtue and a little luck; for Christianity, since your immortal soul is at stake, best to leave the job to an expert (God).

3. The highest moral act is love of God for his own sake.

UP FOR GRABS

1. Are the virtues connected or unified somehow? If so, how much? Is there a 'master-virtue' the attainment of which leads us to develop all others?

2. Which is more important for being virtuous: intellect or will? (For example: Can you have highly developed prudence and yet still be wicked?)

3. Can pagans be morally virtuous? Can virtuous pagans go to heaven?

4. How can we explain the moral virtue of the saints? If they are so very good because of divine grace or because their own saintly nature, then they never have had to work at being good, as do the rest of us. Do they really deserve praise, then? While we admire the strength of a lion, we don't praise the lion for it, since it is natural.

5. In the moral development of the individual Christian, do the moral virtues depend on the theological virtues?

6. Do external factors play a significant role in determining whether an action is moral or not? Or is the most important factor instead the internal dimension, say, the intentions behind the act?

Ockham and Moral Luck

While Ockham had strong views on all of the issues that were up for grabs, not all these opinions were controversial. In his 1319 work *On the Connection of the Virtues*, he organized his ethical theory around a complex stratification of virtues and vices into five distinct grades, partly following a somewhat similar arrangement he encountered reading Aristotle's *Ethics* and which he commented on around 1318. Using this five-grade scheme, he developed nuanced answers to all of the contentious questions 1–6 listed above, continuing to defend these ideas up through the early 1320s. For example, in regard to up-for-grabs item 2, although he recognized the importance of rightly functioning practical intellect (prudence) in moral activity, following general Franciscan predilection he tended rather to stress the importance of the will in moral actions. One implication of this emphasis has consequences for item 4. Ockham made it clear that, to the extent that we think saints and martyrs are morally praiseworthy, to that same extent we must be sure not to attribute to them motives and moral habits so strong that these things causally determine their free will, and so eclipse it.

As interesting as these views are, we will proceed in a less specifically theological vein, and explore one philosophically interesting aspect of his focus on the will, namely, his insistent and controversial response to item 6 immediately above. Ockham famously held that, in moral assessment, only factors internal to the agent matter, viz., the intellect but also and especially the *motives* underlying the will. External factors are accidental, outside the agent's control, and hence play no role in moral assessment. As Ockham puts it, the interior act alone is sin, or, put the other way, external acts are morally neutral, neither good nor bad. Despite the controversy this particular view engendered on account of its variance from the views of Scotus, the most famous Franciscan theologian of the time, Ockham never seems to have changed his mind about it, and we find him, during this very rocky period of his life, nevertheless defending and clarifying this opinion in his later *Quodlibets*, which records debates that probably occurred just before his arrival in Avignon. Because it was controversial, philosophically interesting, and is connected with important modern discussions of 'moral luck', we will focus on Ockham's claim that only a person's will and intentions are properly morally praised or blamed.

Consider two women, Alice and Barbara, each on her way to the local Oxford church on a steel-gray Sunday morning in May, 1324. Are they both being good? Ockham says that we first must ask whether both Alice and Barbara are following *right reason*, that is, a correctly functioning intellect, giving sound moral advice according to some correct percept, say, 'One ought to go to church on Sunday'. Let us suppose that in fact Alice and Barbara each have this percept in mind and are following it when first they leave home. This percept of right reason, Ockham would say, is a partial object of their wills, that is, it is in each case a part of the overall aim in going to church. So far in the example we see that Alice and Barbara are equivalent in *external actions*, i.e., moving their bodies down the stone lane toward the church, and they are also *intellectually equivalent*, having as a partial object the (let's assume) correct moral percept 'One ought to go to church on Sunday'. But this is only the first stage of the analysis; knowing only this much, we cannot yet say if they are both being good.

For consider, Ockham would argue, what would happen if halfway to the church Alice suddenly thinks that she may see her adulterous lover there; she flushes, quickening her step to match her racing heart. Barbara, let us assume, continues to walk as before under the desire to praise God and to fulfill the percept previously mentioned. Alice now has a new partial object for her will, 'To see fair young John Smith', and Barbara has now thought of praising God, so her will has also changed it object. Clearly now there is some moral difference between them. But their mere intellects and the basic forward movements of their bodies are the same, so if we had to judge them solely on these bases we could recognize no important difference. Or rather, we might even interpret Alice's movements as pious zeal for worship, and so (incorrectly) judge her as being slightly better than Barbara. Ockham's take is that looking at intellect and externals alone really tells us nothing about the morality of the actors, and, taking the point characteristically to its extreme, Ockham concludes that in fact, the *external action* of going to church, say, cannot properly speaking be said to be good or bad, because it can be done with good or with evil intent equally. Only what is in the heart ultimately matters in moral evaluation.

This insistence on the primacy of the will works the other way as well. Suppose the next day John Smith and Alice are (separately) going to confession sincerely to repent their relationship, motivated in part by right reason telling them 'One ought to repent sins' and 'Adultery is a sin'. But, let us suppose, along the way John is attacked by brigands, robbed, and left injured. Alice, let us assume, succeeds in confessing. In this case, John had bad moral luck; his intentions were good, but his body was prevented by external forces from completing his internal intentions. The spirit was willing, but the flesh was waylaid. Ockham would not allow the external events, the accidental bad moral luck, to affect our moral assessment of John. Since he was following exactly the same percept of right reason as Alice and had similarly sincere intent, he was, in heading to confession, being just as good as Alice was, although only Alice made it to confession. There is not such thing, Ockham thought, as moral luck.

I used an example of two people going off to confession on purpose, because it illustrates a theological danger inherent in Ockham's view. For consider, as noted above, in Catholicism (or any sacramental religious system), rites such as baptism or confession are supposed to have actual spiritual power to bring about with divine aid actual spiritual effects that cannot be achieved by any other method. In short, the sacraments are supposed to be efficacious when done properly, and seem to be necessary to rectify the human to the divine. Moreover, it is a short leap from Ockham's conclusion above—that John and Alice are morally equivalent because internally equivalent, forget about the exter-

nals—to the conclusion that it isn't *going* to confession that matters morally, but merely *intending* to go. However, if these last two
are equivalent, then it suggests that the rite of confession itself is
not strictly necessary. But then neither are confessionals. Nor
priests, perhaps, since intending to take part in a sacrament is
enough to get the benefit ordinarily conferred by the rite.
According to a criticism made by Chatton, when taken to the theological extreme, this view entails that Jesus didn't have to be crucified to save humanity, he just had to intend to be crucified. The
crucifixion itself would be superfluous.

This last remark is not fair, perhaps, and we don't know how
Ockham would have responded to it, because by the time it was
made, he was already outside the intellectual community of Oxford
for good. Still, his views on this matter were uncompromising, and
did have strong consequences, which he nevertheless did not
shrink from. But Ockham's insistence on intellectual consistency
over orthodox compromise could not have come at a worse time.

Ockham Is Drawn into the
Poverty Controversy

It is fitting that we ended this discussion of epistemology and
ethics by talking about moral luck, because luck seems to have
played a large and damning role in the outcome of Ockham's stay
in Avignon—but maybe not in the way you would imagine. He
was eventually cleared on the charges that originally brought him
there, receiving some censure, but no formal condemnation for
heretical content. Despite his unrepentant attitude and the realist
predilections of his examiners, it seems that the *venerabilis inceptor* had walked the line finely enough to remain on the sunny side
of the doctrinal divide. But if he was cleared of heresy, why did he
later have to run away from Avignon?

Just when all looked well for our hero, fate moved against him.
Or rather: someone who did not understand Ockham's combative
character well enough (or did he understand it too well?) asked
him to weigh in on an issue that had recently become a terrible
sore spot between the Pope and the Franciscans. Moreover, this
was someone to whom Ockham owed direct obedience. The
somewhat predictable result was that Ockham, already in town
under dark auspices and not knowing when to quit, behaved very

much in character, and said plainly what he thought about the controversy, having duly sifted the evidence. The someone who drew him in was Michael of Cesena, Minister General of the Franciscan Order, and the issue he was drawn into has come to be known today as the Franciscan poverty controversy.

8

The Exile in Munich
(1328–1347)

OCKHAM'S POLITICAL THEORY

It's difficult to escape the feeling that Ockham almost made it out of Avignon in safety. Although he was aware of the poverty controversy when it began to heat up in 1323, he managed to stay clear of it for almost all of his time in Avignon. He later wrote that he had been living in Avignon almost four years before he was drawn into it and so into open conflict with Pope John XXII (d. 1334).

Since he originally left *for* Avignon in May of 1324 and subsequently ran *from* Avignon in May of 1328, a total of four years in itself, it follows that his entanglement with and break from John XXII came only at the end of his stay, and it was evidently precipitous and grave. What occasioned all this trouble? Since not only the impetus for but also the content of Ockham's political theories have the poverty controversy at their root, we must first look into the history and structure of that conflict. Only then will we be able to make sense of these tumultuous events and the philosophical response they elicited from Ockham.

The Poverty Controversy

The Franciscans, as a preaching order devoted to teaching about Christianity in part by example, had attempted from their inception to model the first-century activities of Jesus and the Apostles as they imagined them, and so upheld a very serious ideal of communal living and of mendicant poverty. As individuals they owned no property—no land, no animals, no machinery, no tools, no mechanisms of conveyance, no slaves, nor even food and clothing.

Each friar renounced ownership of all worldly things upon taking full vows in the Order, and instead lived communally and simply, accepting donations and alms from laity, and working together with his fellows to meet the basic needs of life and do the work of the Order. This meant that the practice of poverty was, for them, not simply a general spiritual ideal, but was an *imitation of Christ.* Considered thus far, by itself, Franciscan poverty seems noble and uncontroversial, although it always caused some tension with the central ecclesiastical hierarchy, who necessarily used money and property in the vast administrative activities of the Church. This tension might have simply continued at a low level, without eruption, but for two additional factors.

First, add the fact that during Ockham's life the papacy was in a particularly acute 'worldly phase', moving itself north (in 1309) from Rome to Avignon, there amassing great material wealth and asserting more influence over secular affairs in northern Europe. (Some people today even call this 'the Babylonian captivity' of the papacy.) Imagine the juxtaposition of papal opulence and power against Franciscan poverty, in a religion whose own founder uttered many sharp criticisms of excess wealth and many tender words for the poor and powerless. The condition of the papacy therefore contributed to an increase in the tension, and it might have been a good time for the Franciscans not to make too much noise about their vaunted poverty ideal.

But this did not happen. Concurrent with this papal opulence was a rising debate within the Order itself about the interpretation of the poverty vows. According to the strict intent of St. Francis himself, the Franciscans should proclaim complete poverty, not only as individuals (as explained above), *but also as a group.* The view was that they not only gave up personal property and ownership when joining the Franciscans, but that, upon joining, they did not thereby take on even *joint* ownership of the accompaniments to their daily communal life. By the fourteenth century this included a considerable list of items: the food they ate, the convent buildings they slept in, the land those buildings sat on, the *studia* they trained in at Oxford, London, and all over Europe, and even their crowded and widely envied libraries. But if no individual Franciscan owned these important items, and if the local chapters did not own them communally, nor the Franciscan Order as a whole, who did own them?

The Franciscan answer to the question was this: the pope—not as a person, but as the leader of the Holy See—owns it all for us.

Early in Franciscan history (the Order was founded in 1209), when they were a small group, the popes made an arrangement whereby the Franciscans did not own property communally, and instead certain members of the papal court were appointed to 'officially' own the property the friars used, making them free to make use of many things, while leaving their communal and individual poverty intact. This arrangement was even upheld at various points through the late thirteenth century in certain official papal pronouncements (called 'Bulls'). As the Order grew, strict observance of the rule of communal poverty became less and less practical, of course, and there were some Franciscans (called 'conventuals') who resented the difficulties this situation entailed, and who believed that merely individual poverty was good enough. After all, the other intellectually dominant preaching group of the time, the Dominican Order, observed only individual poverty, not communal poverty. At the beginning of the fourteenth century, the problem began to quicken, because some of those Franciscans who opposed the compromise position of the conventuals (the so-called 'spirituals'), made the controversy vivid by insisting that mendicant poverty was a *literal* imitation of Christ, not an approximation of an ideal, because (they claimed), as a matter of historical fact, Jesus and his disciples practiced both individual *and* communal poverty.

The conjunction of this internal fighting with papal extravagance could not have been more badly timed, because it seemed to cast unfavorable light on the material power of the papacy. Tensions with the popes increased. In 1316 Michael of Cesena, a moderate conventual, was elected minister general of the Franciscan Order to try to mollify the demands of the spirituals but still keep good relations with the papacy. This was a difficult task at best, but it was made almost impossible by the crisis that broke when newly elected (1316) John XXII began to act vigorously to end the poverty dispute once and for all. Michael's lack of success can be inferred from the fact that, several years later, in an important Bull in 1323 John XXII essentially rescinded the arrangement whereby the papacy managed the property the Franciscans used. Why he ultimately broke with the tradition of support in this way, undermining a pillar of Franciscan piety, is not entirely clear. Possibly, under the influence of criticisms of the Avignon style of religious rule, he sensed a politically dangerous implication in this uncompromising attitude of the spirituals, which could be interpreted this way: *the Franciscans* couldn't own anything because they were too busy imitating Christ (and getting pretty close at that) but *the Pope* could help them continue by holding title to their stuff, all with no appreciable loss of piety for him and his office, since they were already so deeply in league with mammon anyway. All Franciscans, but especially Michael of Cesena, the man in charge, were horrified at this withdrawal of previous papal support for their communal poverty.

Michael was in the Papal Court in Avignon in 1323 when this controversial Bull came out. Over the next few years he worked with increasing desperation, but little effect, to alter Pope John XXII's thinking on the issue. As Michael made his arguments, the Pope only did more damage by issuing several new Bulls denouncing Franciscan communal poverty as illogical, impossible, and without scriptural basis, thereby raising some difficult questions about the practice. For example, he argued that either the Franciscans had some legal right to such items as the food they ate and clothes they wore, in some sense of the word 'right', or else they did not. If they did not, then they were no better than thieves who steal their food and clothes, and so they would be unjust. If they do have a right to these things, then they do so either by way of communal ownership or individual ownership; but either way would go against their customs and their self-concept. It seemed that this showdown in Avignon must inevitably lead to a break between the Pope and the conventuals, on the one side, and the spirituals, on the other.

But into Michael's troubling situation a new hope arrived. As we have already seen, right around this time, a young English Franciscan theologian named William had arrived in town on entirely different business. But nevertheless, there he was, a man obedient to the Order, stubborn, opinionated, accustomed to controversy, and *almost unmatched in logical argument*. Sometime in late 1327 or 1328, Michael must have turned to Ockham as a final hope to try to rally support and roll things back to the way they were.

Ockham's own description of what happened next is so perfect, and so perfectly Ockham, that I will simply quote him at length from John Kilcullen's translation:

Presently, however, when some occasion arose, at the command of a superior [Michael] I read and diligently studied three of his constitutions [= John XXII's Bulls] . . . In these I found a great many things that were heretical, erroneous, silly, ridiculous, fantastic, insane, and defamatory, contrary and likewise plainly adverse to orthodox faith, good morals, natural reason, certain experience, and fraternal charity. (*A Letter to the Friars Minor*, p. 3)

The diligent reader may notice that at the end of this passage Ockham condemns John XXII by citing, among others, the three sources of authority listed in his razor: religion, reason, and certain experience.

After listing in detail precisely those claims he regards as heretical, insane, and so on, Ockham continues, in a passage that captures his philosophical personality about as well as anything he ever wrote:

Let no one think, therefore, that because of the multitude of this pseudo-popes's supporters or because of arguments that are common to heretics and to the orthodox, I would wish to abandon acknowledged truth. For I prefer the divine Scriptures to a man who is a simpleton in sacred literature, and I prefer the teaching of the holy fathers reigning with Christ to the deliverances of those living in this mortal life. . . . But if someone shows me plainly that the constitutions and sermons of the pseudo-pope do not deviate from Catholic truth, or, alternatively, that one should obey an heretical pope knowing that he is a heretic, I will not be slow to return to the brothers who support him. No one, however, who can prove neither of these things either by argument or by authorities should be hostile either to me or to anyone who does not obey the said heretic. (p. 13)

Ockham wrote this description in retrospect, in the spring of 1334, six years after the events they describe in Avignon in 1328. But even at that earlier time, before exile had woven their fortunes together, Ockham had firmly chosen to side with Michael and his party against the Pope, and he had openly stated pretty much the same opinions; this is why he had to pack his duds and scoot.

And so we have come full circle; we arrive back at our starting point, May 26th, 1328, dead of night, at the papal residence in Avignon, preparing to steal the official seal of the Order. As Ockham prepared to leave the city and his ecclesiastical career behind, he may have guessed that he would subsequently be excommunicated, but he may not have thought that he would also leave behind his great achievements in logic and metaphysics. Not that Ockham reversed himself philosophically; on the contrary, we have no evidence to suggest that he changed his mind on nominalism or ethics or logic during his exile. Rather, he seems to have turned his back on metaphysics entirely after Avignon, and devoted his remaining years to battling with the Pope, and more astonishingly, with the *papacy*. Ockham in effect challenged the entire medieval concept of church-state relations, and kept the pressure up throughout the remainder of his life.

Why he widened his attack from arguing about the small (but personally important) context of the Franciscan poverty controversy to questioning systematically one of the most fundamental relationships in medieval society—sacred versus secular rule—we can only speculate. But it does fit very nicely with the stubborn intellectual courage we have come to see in his other debates.

From *The Work of Ninety Days* to *Eight Questions on the Power of the Pope*

Now excommunicated for leaving Avignon without permission, and in exile lest he be imprisoned, Ockham sought protection first in Pisa, thereafter in Munich, under the patronage of Louis of Bavaria, who was Holy Roman Emperor, and no fan of John XXII. Other than *The Letter to the Friars Minor* (quoted from above) and several shorter works, he wrote two major treatises on political theory before he died, *The Work of Ninety Days* and the unfinished *Dialogus*. The *Dialogus* is enormous, and is still being edited from manuscripts. Hence, in this section we will look into his edited works to see how the issues surrounding the poverty controversy, addressed in *The Work of Ninety Days* in the early 1330s, led from a theory of rights to a sophisticated, dualistic theory of power-sharing between church and state in a short work called *Eight Questions on the Power of the Pope*, written around 1340.

Natural Rights in *The Work of Ninety Days*

Ockham's philosophical defense of Franciscan poverty evolved from—what else?—a carefully described set of distinctions about the use of two Latin terms, *dominium* (= lordship, dominion; a basic control or command over something) and *ius* (= a right). The term *dominium*, Ockham insisted, has at least two species, exclusive and non-exclusive. Non-exclusive *dominium* (I will translate this from now on as 'lordship') amounts to a kind of common, open, or joint control over something, for example, the air we all breath is legitimately used by you and by me too; I have lordship enough to legitimately take the air of this world into my lungs for my own use, and so do you. But this is not exclusive to me; every atom belonging to me as good belongs to you. And notice, my lordship of air would be non-exclusive even if I were the only air-breathing creature on earth; being the (contingently) sole user of thing over which I have lordship is still not exclusive lordship; the air would still not be in any deep sense *my own* just because I'm the only one who happens to be using it right now. Exclusive lordship, by contrast, amounts to what we usually call 'ownership' in English. If I have exclusive lordship over a house, then nobody rightly lays hold of it save for me.

Similarly, there are two kinds of *ius*, or rights: *ius fori*, or *ius poli*. We could translate *ius fori* as 'legal right'. A *ius fori* is a right granted by human law: for example, in certain countries citizens have a right to health care; or consider property rights, which are established and maintained by deeds and titles. A *ius poli* is something more like a 'natural right,' although Ockham thought of it more theologically, as a right of heaven, a God-granted basic right to use things in accordance with natural moral laws. For example, even in the absence of any specific legal rights, we have a *ius poli* to defend our bodies from unjustifiable attack.

Now, Michael of Cesena, in defending Franciscan poverty as an imitation of Christ, suggested that Jesus and his disciples treated the material goods in their lives, not as property, but as things simply available for their use, including even those things they used up by using them at all (such as food and clothing). In this way, their use reflected a genuine and profound poverty, bypassing and in effect rejecting the human institutions of money and private ownership. Jesus and the twelve disciples had created in Palestine the conditions existing in the Garden of Eden before Adam's exile, a time before human institutions created private property and money. The Franciscans in Ockham's time were simply carrying forward that ancient tradition, enjoying the simple use of the things of this world without owning those things, individually or collectively.

John XXII responded to Michael's line of reasoning by saying that in fact property rights already existed in the Garden before the exile, because while still in paradise, God told Adam he had lordship or dominion (= *dominium*) over the earth. Thus we have it on the authority of Genesis that Adam was in effect the world's first owner. Hence, John XXII reasoned there never was a natural state of the world without dominion or lordship to which Jesus could have returned, and so the Franciscans certainly could not claim his behavior as a precedent for theirs.

Ockham's response to this Papal argument was to point out that not all lordship is exclusive. Genesis is correct, of course; Adam had lordship in the Garden, but not the exclusive lordship of ownership. Rather, he had non-exclusive lordship; even Adam's solitude (before the creation of Eve) did not entail exclusive ownership, but only a kind of general, non-exclusive stewardship in perpetuity, not just for him but also for all his descendents. Adam did not have to leave the world to the rest of us in his will or anything such thing. God's command in Genesis to 'have dominion' does not mean 'It's all yours, Adam,' and so does not refute the Franciscan view.

However, John XXII had extended his attack beyond this basic objection from *dominium* by appealing to a principle of Roman law that seems clearly to have applied to Franciscan poverty: according to that law, no one could use a thing in such a way that its substance is destroyed unless that person has right (= *ius*) to it, which right is obviously conveyed by law through ownership. Since the Franciscans claimed not to own anything, not even as a group, they did not have rights over anything, including their food or clothing. But food, clothing, and other personal items, are consumed in use, and so their substance is destroyed in use. Since the Franciscans were using such consumables without ownership and hence without a right, they were using things such as food and clothing unjustly.

At this stage of the argument Ockham turned to his claim that there are two kinds of *ius* or rights, the legal rights that are instituted by human law courts (= *ius fori*) and those that are natural, general and God-granted (= *ius poli*). The latter always existed, even before human society became complex and difficult, but they eventually had to be suspended and superseded by the former. Hence by a natural right (= *ius poli*) that flowed from his non-exclusive lordship, Adam used things in the Garden of Eden, even consumable things like food. After the exile, with the growing human population, limits and boundaries had to be invented and maintained, so institutions such as property and exclusive lordship were invented as legal rights (= *ius fori*). Since the right to use what I need by natural rights is clearly incompatible with other people's legal rights (for example, I cannot use your car and your home by my natural right), we must admit that, since the exile from the Garden, natural rights are suspended, though not destroyed, and have been replaced by the more specific and limiting human decrees that define legal rights.

Ockham pulls all this together to refute John XXII as follows. When the Pope said that the Franciscans must have a right to use things that are consumed in use to use them justly, he was correct. But he was wrong to suppose that the only way for the Franciscans to have a right to things like food and clothing is for someone else to transfer ownership to them, and hence to give them a legal right to those goods. For although natural rights are suspended since the exile from paradise, *they still exist, but are not normally operative.* Hence, in order to transfer food and clothing to the Franciscans as a gift, *without also transferring ownership*, it is enough that the owner who gives the gift simply suspends his own legal right to the material object in question. When the giver does this, the previous suspension of the natural right by the legal right is canceled, and so the old natural right operates once again, and the item is essentially up for grabs.

A useful analogy is as follows. Think of a beauty contest with a first place and a second place, in other words a winner and a runner-up. At the end of such a contest, the name of the runner-up is announced first, and at that point, and for a brief moment, she is the highest-ranking contestant in the competition. Her claim to being highest is swiftly eclipsed by the announcement of the winner, of course, who then takes the crown. But the claim of the runner-up to the crown does not go away completely; all that is necessary for the runner-up to reclaim her place as first (and so to claim even the crown), is for the winner to relinquish her own claim; immediately the dormant claim of the runner-up reemerges and becomes operative. Just so, when a donor gives the Franciscans something, if in doing so she simply relinquishes her legal claim, which claim previously eclipsed the natural right of use, straightaway the natural right of use returns and becomes operative.

At this point the Franciscans would then be free to assert this natural right, to take the thing and use it, even to use it up. The only caveat is that since the natural right is outside of human law, the Franciscans did not have any recourse if the giver changed her mind and took the gift back. They could not sue or protest legally, for this would imply that their use of the gift was bound up with some *legal right* to it, and so would imply *exclusive lordship* over the thing. But, barring this, their exercise of the natural right over the gift, even if it were something consumable in use, never rose to the level of exclusive lordship, and so was not ownership, and implied no legal rights at all. The Franciscans, Ockham asserted, remained in poverty.

Ockham's tidy solution to John XXII's argument against Franciscan poverty depends upon a strong notion of natural rights, and that these rights are thought of as built in to the human situation by God. This in itself is an exciting concept, anticipating in some way the modern concept of human rights. But in his solution Ockham also acknowledges man-made legal rights, which are created and enforced by secular princes and law courts. Thus his theory contains at its center a bifurcation of political legitimacy into two domains – secular and sacred. It turns out that this split was also vital to his more mature political theory, and the use he made of it strikes many people as thoroughly modern. Perhaps it is even his greatest contribution to history and to human thought apart from metaphysical theorizing. The best place to see it developed is in his *Eight Questions on the Power of the Pope*.

Political Dualism in *Eight Questions*

The ancient Spartans famously had a unusual system of governance in which there were two kings. One king ruled in matters of peace and domestic affairs: punishment of lawbreakers, taxation, etc. The other ruled in matters of war—leading troops, assigning commanders, putting down slave revolts, convincing colonies to obey. Today this system might strike us as somewhat unlikely, because we tend assume that good governance depends upon an essentially united locus of political authority; whatever checks are imposed on a government and however internally pluralistic it is, the country it rules can have only one highest authority, and so only one king. We think this even of modern parliamentary systems in which kings and queens are only figureheads. Thus, although modern Britain has a Home Secretary and a Defense Minister and an Exchequer, all of them answer to *the* Prime Minister, and this makes sense to us. If it were otherwise, it seems government would consist of two or more 'supreme' rulers, seeking always to best one another, and this would lead to civil war instead of unity and prosperity. Let us use the term *political monism* to refer to the presumption that kingship over people is best if strictly monarchical, that is if a single locus of power sits supreme as the final authority for settling disputes.

Like the Spartans, Ockham rejected political monism in favor of a rich and complex dualism. Unlike the Spartans, however, Ockham did not divide the burden of rule into domestic/peacetime affairs on the one side, and foreign/wartime affairs on the other. Rather, he started with a dualism that was more natural to the Middle Ages: spiritual affairs versus secular affairs. Over the first Ockham would set a single spiritual king to govern the church and its functions—someone like a pope—and over the latter he would set a secular king to govern the secular state in temporal affairs. In order for his system to remain a true dualism, Ockham must not only argue that two rulers are better than one, but also that neither ruler should be subordinated to the other; not the king to the pope (as so often happened in the mediaeval world), nor yet the pope to the king (as tends to happen in modern liberal democracies).

Although in many respects his ideas reflected a conservative medieval world view, in the fourteenth century Ockham nevertheless advocated something we regard as thoroughly modern: church-state separation. As Ockham puts it:

> . . . neither the pope nor the Roman Church has by Christ's institution power regularly to entrust temporal jurisdictions to the emperor and other secular rulers, and they can exercise them without his commission. (Kilcullen, p. 308)

In short, the emperor does not depend upon the pope for his legitimacy. This goes beyond the mere distinction of legal and natural rights, as above, for it makes the normative claim that secular power does not have to answer absolutely to the church. Not only are the legal and secular different from the sacred, they are in fact best ruled differently as well. Why does he think this?

Given his experiences in the poverty controversy, it will cause no surprise to learn that Ockham's primary concern in governance was with the abuse of power. For although some central power is necessary in human affairs, in order to prevent discord in the community, nevertheless

> . . . no community of persons able to have discords among themselves would be best ordered if it were subject regularly and in every case to one supreme judge; for in such a community the supreme judge could do wrong with impunity, to the destruction of the whole community, and this conflicts with the best ordering of any community. (Kilcullen, p. 310)

Thus Ockham is advocating, not only an idea of separation of power, but also of checks and balances. Although it's easy to overstate the modern tone of his political thought (we should remember that he does not advocate elections or democracy, for example) nevertheless it seems that Ockham was on the verge of something great, and was again ahead of his times.

However we ultimately assess Ockham's role in this controversy, the wider historical significance of this conflict is difficult to overstate. To sum up and draw out that significance, we need only note that the loss of prestige to the papacy occasioned by this high-profile exchange was surely the partial background for the Reformation, 150 years later. What may seem like a very recondite and technical exchange between two highly trained, stubborn churchmen actually had an enormous impact, if not on the world of ideas (since church-state separation did not catch on for a long time!), then certainly on the history of Christianity. Moreover, Ockham continued his unrelenting attacks on this issue, writing ever grander treatises on faith, reason, and political authority through the remainder of his life.

Did Ockham Recant?

Even the great ones pass, and so with Ockham. We have only a little hard evidence about the general circumstances of his death. We know that he died in Munich, and that his protector, Louis of

Bavaria, Holy Roman Emperor, died in a hunting accident in the spring of 1347. For many years it was assumed that Ockham died two years after his patron, in 1349, despite some other evidence that he died in 1347. For a long time the 1349 date was the one we believed. There were two reasons to suppose this 1349 date was correct.

First, 1348–49 was an almost unbelievable plague year. Perhaps one-fourth of the population of Europe died. Even the *doctor invincibilis* wasn't actually invincible.

Second, we have a letter written on June 8th, 1349, from Pope Clement VI, authorizing the new Minister General of the Franciscan Order, Brother Farina (Michael had been long since removed) to lift all censures on a certain 'William, of England'. This clemency was being granted to 'William' in exchange for his returning the stolen seal of the order to the new Minister General, and submitting himself to the authority of the Pope.

Was the 'William, of England' referred to in the Pope's letter our own William of Ockham, still alive in the summer of 1349, but soon forfeit to a desolate winter of black plague? This identification makes some sense: William of Ockham was from England, of course; he was with the original group of friars who stole the Franciscan seal; it also makes sense that in the face of the blazing epidemic, death all around, Ockham might see a chance at reconciliation with the church and take it. Could this 1349 letter be papal recompense for a deathbed retraction, indicating a successful attempt by Ockham to reverse his excommunication before it was too late? Given the situation, such behavior might be understandable, but still it leaves a bad taste in the mouth—is this the unyielding champion of reason we know and love? Did Ockham really give in at the end?

9

Afterword

OCKHAM'S INFLUENCE AND LEGACY

As it turns out, he didn't recant his position on poverty. In 1982, Gedeon Gál, a Franciscan and an extraordinary Ockham scholar, finally showed in an important paper that we should instead trust the date on Ockham's grave in Munich, which is clearly marked 1347, not 1349. Gál even succeeded in explaining the letter from Clement VI that led to the mistaken idea that Ockham recanted and died in 1349: it seems that there was, in Munich, another English Franciscan named William, one of William Ockham's colleagues, in fact. This *other* William was a renegade originally, but penitent in the end: he returned the Franciscan seal and was rewarded in 1349, but this William was not *our* William of Ockham at all. And of course all this implies that Ockham avoided the Black Death of 1349 by stubbornly dying two years in advance, and that he did so before the seal was returned and so before this amnesty from Clement VI, which was never even directed toward him.

Ockham didn't recant after all. The title of Gál's paper says it best: "William of Ockham Died Impenitent in April 1347."

Although this (now generally accepted) version of his death makes him seem more intellectually heroic perhaps, it probably does not (and will not) really change our estimation of his intellectual contribution one way or the other, for good or for ill. Today Ockham's legacy is quite secure, his reputation as one of the three brightest minds of the later Latin Middle Ages seems unshakable.

Immediate Influence

This is ironic, in a way, because Ockham was not phenomenally influential, even at Oxford, for the first fifty years after his death. He was an important figure, of course, and his nominalism caught the positive interest of some talented Oxonians, for example, Adam Wodeham. But even Wodeham disagreed with many aspects of Ockham's thought, and Ockham's realist critics had just as much influence. There was something of a stalemate between these two camps for the first half of the fourteenth century.

This deadlock was eventually broken, not by philosophy, but by plague and Augustinianism: Oxford was so depopulated by the former that the production of original work in term logic underwent a precipitous decline, lasting right into the early Renaissance, and Oxford was so taken in by the latter that Ockham's stress on the freedom of the will in ethics began to savor of an ancient heresy Augustine combated, called 'Pelagianism'. His influence fell further. Moreover, with Ockham physically out of the way during the intellectually active 1330s, the 1340s saw a rise in the influence of the Oxford realists, led in part by people such as Walter Chatton, who served as Franciscan regent master there during academic year 1329–30.

Fortunately, Ockham-style nominalism had a less ambiguous reception on the continent. After some initial resistance, scholars at the University of Paris showed great interest in Ockham's ideas in logic and metaphysics. This fame spread to other parts of Europe, and, until the general demise of Scholasticism in the Renaissance, his name lent itself to a school of thought, 'Ockhamism', a system characterized by careful attention to philosophy of language and logic, together with a nominalist turn of mind in metaphysics.

Lasting Legacy

Besides the many fascinating philosophical ideas sketched in this book, and others still uncharted, what legacy does Ockham leave for the world of ideas in the twenty-first century? I single out several items of note that transcend the particulars of his historical context:

1. A sketch of grand nominalism. Many philosophers feel that metaphysics sometimes goes too far, but few have ever conceived so vast and systematic a plan to deflate it. Even if the particulars of Ockham's reduction scheme are tied to an Aristotelian system no longer ascendant, still the style of systematic reduction he imagined has been reintroduced with no slight enthusiasm by modern critics in the analytic tradition of philosophy, for example W.V. Quine.

2. A warning not to be bewitched by language. This same message, albeit tinged with some a mysticism not found in Ockham, has been advanced in the modern age by no less a figure than Ludwig Wittgenstein (d. 1951).

3. A message of compatibility between faith and reason that is neither soaked with compromise nor fired by extremism. Ockham seems to have suggested in his general approach to theology that it is acceptable to attempt to justify with reason what is believed by faith, and it is also acceptable to fail in this attempt.

4. A sober appraisal of the advantage of a division between church and state. Although he likely would not have approved of the religious pluralism that succeeded upon this idea in the United States for example (however much we who enjoy pluralism may approve of it), nevertheless Ockham deserves credit for a rigorous development of church-state division at a crucial time in Western history.

But in my view his greatest legacy is the strange and interesting example of his life, not only his views but also his deeds, and the philosophical personality that informed them. How, though, can this personality be squared with the rest of his modern reputation? How should the reader of this book, who now has a sense of Ockham's most important views, understand his contribution to the world of ideas? Should he be seen as a man out of his time, a harbinger of modernity, a destroyer of Aquinas's earlier faith-reason synthesis, or one of the finest philosophers of the longest period in the history of philosophy?

My opinion on this subject, which the reader is now in a position to assess, is that Ockham's philosophical reputation is deserved, but that his philosophical personality is generally misunderstood by modern people, since it is a confluence of streams that we think of as inconsistent today: deep religiosity, together with an absolute regard for the highest possible standards of evidence. Modern people tend to focus on one side or the other, and then praise or criticize him according to their own preconceptions. In order to make the point, I hope I may be forgiven if I briefly caricature the extremes of these preconceptions.

Modern educated secular people view deep religiosity and high standards of evidence as fundamentally incompatible, and they prefer the latter. Consequently, to the extent that they know only Ockham's hard-headed nominalism, usually through some bastardized version of his razor, such people wrongly think him a misunderstood promethean hero of proto-science, living in an historical epoch of intolerance and irrationality. If ever they learn of his confrontation with the papacy, this view is at once confirmed. By contrast, to the extent that secular people know Ockham only as a medieval theologian, they will often not give his views a chance, assuming as they must that a man of religious feeling and conviction is not rigorous, and so not worth a look philosophically. Those secular people who manage to put both sides of Ockham together can only downplay one facet or the other, or else write him off as a mystery of schizoid intellectual compartmentalization.

Modern and moderate religious people hope that deep religiosity and high standards of evidence are fundamentally compatible, but they often lack the philosophical and theological training to verify this hope for themselves, and the audacity to see the attempt through wherever it may lead. For such people Ockham's example can be a worry, for the paths of his investigations led to strange ideas, social rejection, and career implosion.

Modern Christian fideists and fundamentalists don't care if religion is compatible with anything, provided they themselves go to heaven. To these Ockham must seem merely a cautionary example, if they are Catholic, or an early Reformer of the corrupt papacy if they are Protestant. Ockham's stress on divine omnipotence in the debate over absolute/ordained power (Chapter 5), and also his political views (Chapter 8), often bolster this latter view of Ockham as proto-Reformer.

But having now had Ockham explained to her, the reader of this book can see for herself: the truth of Ockham is subject nei-

ther to the fission of the secularists and fideists, nor to the hesita-
tion of the religious moderates. One of the best logicians of his
day, he nevertheless cheerfully admits the limits of reason; a devout
friar in the heyday of Franciscan revitalization of Catholicism, he
nevertheless declares the Pope a heretic and suggests church-state
separation.

The resolution to this paradox, if it is a resolution at all, lies in
Ockham's courage and in his candor. He would not budge on the
fundamentals of his theologically informed metaphysics, but where
other philosopher-theologians would stretch the evidence of reason to achieve a seemingly satisfying metaphysical account, he
would not bend, but rather tended to confess his own ignorance
and to point out the ignorance of others, a thing not unamusing
to witness. More than anything else, Ockham was a paragon of
intellectual vigor, someone good to know, even today.

Glossary

These glosses are meant as an aid for the reader who has finished Chapter 3; see the discussion in the body of the text for fuller explanations and more examples. The entries are technical vocabulary from Ockham's logic. The meanings are meant to apply to Ockham and are not necessarily general; some medieval authors used these same words very differently. [I am indebted to item 4 in the bibliography below for the formulations of the definitions under 'supposition'.]

absolute terms. Generally speaking, terms that have a real definition, and which signify all the things that they signify equally, for example, 'animal', 'stone' [contrast with **connotative terms**].

categorematic terms. Terms that have a definite, finite signification, usually category words; for example, 'man', 'white' [contrast with **syncategorematic terms**].

connotative terms. Terms that have a only a nominal definition, and which signify the things that they signify unequally, for example, signifying a thing and connoting its manner of existence, for example, 'white', 'similar' [contrast with **absolute terms**].

definition

    nominal definition. A definition of a term that merely records how the term is used, as though the term were simply an abbreviation of the definition itself; connotative terms only have definitions of this kind.

    real definition. A definition of a term that records some deep metaphysical fact about the thing the term signifies; only absolute terms have definitions of this kind.

imposition

    first imposition. The first, most basic use of spoken and written terms: to pick out and talk about non-linguistic things in the world; for example, 'tiger', 'fire', 'this great idea I just had'.

second imposition. The secondary, derivative use of spoken and written terms: to pick out, organize, and talk about language itself; for example, 'noun', 'second imposition', 'disyllable'.

intention

first intention. Terms of first imposition that refer to objects outside the mind; for example, 'tiger'.

second intention. Terms of first imposition that refer to objects inside the mind, that is, to concepts, ideas or other mental events; for example, 'this great idea I just had', 'universals'.

mental language. The language of human thought, shared by all people; one of the three levels of language, the other two being spoken and written.

signification. A term signifies all those things it causes us to think of; categorematic terms have clear, finite signification.

supposition. Roughly, the reference a term has as it is used in a proposition; there are at least three important varieties of supposition, which are mutually exclusive:

material supposition. Roughly, the supposition a categorematic term has when it refers to its own spoken or written sign; for example, the term 'man' in 'Man has three letters'. More generally and precisely, the supposition a term has when it refers to a spoken or written expression it does not signify.

personal supposition. The supposition a categorematic term has when it refers to what it signifies, that is, the things it normally calls to mind; for example, the term 'man' in 'Socrates is a man'.

simple supposition. Roughly, the supposition a categorematic term has when it refers to its corresponding mental term; for example, the term 'man' in 'Man is a species,' (that is, 'Man is a species concept'). More generally and precisely, the supposition a term has when it refers to a concept it does not signify.

syncategorematic terms. Terms that do not signify anything on their own, but are significant only in conjunction with other terms, in particular with categorematic terms; for example, 'some', 'only', 'insofar as' [contrast with **categorematic terms**].

terms. Logically significant constituent elements of a proposition.

What to Read Next

This annotated bibliography is aimed at the general reader, and has two parts: first, some general studies on Ockham, second, important translations. Since *Ockham Explained* has no footnote citations, I will take this opportunity to say a few words here by way of acknowledging my debts to the work of my learned colleagues. I used items 1, 2, and 4 constantly. The introductions of most of the translations listed below were also very useful to me, especially item 6. I have drawn on many of the other texts in this list at least once.

Someone otherwise unacquainted with Ockham and medieval philosophy interested in reading further might want to begin with items 3 and 4 below (these are the most accessible commentaries, and item 4 is available online), and also with items 5 and 9 below (these are the most basic English translations from Latin texts; item 5 is by a student of Ockham's, item 9 is by Ockham himself).

General Studies

1. Adams, Marilyn McCord. *William Ockham*. 2 vols. University of Notre Dame Press, 1987.

   The most comprehensive study of Ockham's philosophy and theology in existence. Quite dense and technical for a beginner, but you'll find almost any subject you want to know about discussed here.

2. *The Cambridge Companion to Ockham*. Edited by Paul Vincent Spade. Cambridge University Press, 1999.

   Articles by specialists, sometimes quite technical, but generally readable. It contains an excellent selective bibliography of works on Ockham.

3. Maurer, Armand. *The Philosophy of William Ockham in the Light of Its Principles*. Pontifical Institute of Mediaeval Studies, 1999.

   A very good, comprehensive, and accessible study of Ockham's non-political philosophy. Maurer focuses on the origin of

Ockham's philosophy as a reaction to the work of Scotus far more than does *Ockham Explained*, and so is nicely complimentary to this book. Extensive bibliography.

4. Spade, Paul Vincent, "William of Ockham," in *The Stanford Encyclopedia of Philosophy* (Fall 2006 Edition), edited by Edward N. Zalta, <http://plato.stanford.edu/archives/fall2006/entries/ockham/>.

   Very readable yet compact introduction to Ockham's thought. Includes a bibliography, and links to related articles in the *Stanford Encyclopedia*. The *Stanford Encyclopedia*, available entirely online for no charge and no need to login, is a great place to learn about other figures mentioned in the book; for example, see these entries: "Walter Chatton," "Walter Burley," "Peter Auriol," "John Duns Scotus," "Saint Thomas Aquinas." The table of contents appears at <http://plato.stanford.edu/contents.html>.

English Translations

5. *A Compendium of Ockham's Teachings*. Translated by Julian Davies, OFM. The Franciscan Institute, 1998.

   Not by Ockham himself, but probably written by a devoted follower. It tries to summarize all of Ockham's philosophical views by showing how they follow from just two ideas: (1) divine omnipotence, and (2) the razor.

6. *A Letter to the Friars Minor and Other Writings*. Edited by Arthur Stephen McGrade and John Kilcullen. Translated by John Kilcullen. Cambridge University Press, 1995.

   Go here to read Ockham's political theory.

7. *Ockham on Aristotle's Physics*. Translated by Julian Davies, OFM. The Franciscan Institute, 1989.

   This book translates Ockham's most accessible commentary on Aristotle's *Physics*.

8. *Ockham on the Virtues*. Translated by Rega Wood. Purdue University Press, 1997.

   One of Ockham's most comprehensive discussions of virtue.

9. *Ockham: Philosophical Writings.* Edited by Philotheus Boehner, OFM, revised by Stephen F. Brown. Hackett, 1990.

A classic text and a great place to begin your Ockham collection. Boehner tried to bring central Ockhamist ideas from a variety of texts into one short, cheap English volume.

10. *Ockham's Theory of Terms.* Translated by Michael Loux. St. Augustine Press, 1998.

A translation of Part I of *Summa logicae,* including Ockham's most mature ideas on the theory of terms, but also, if read carefully, a defense of his nominalism.

11. *Predestination, God's Foreknowledge, and Future Contingents.* Translated by Marilyn McCord Adams and Norman Kretzmann. Hackett, 1983.

A complex topic not discussed in this book, but representative of Ockham working to solve philosophical and theological problems using his logic.

12. *William of Ockham Quodlibetal Questions.* Translated by Alfred J Freddoso and Francis E. Kelley. Yale University Press, 1991.

A gem. It contains short discussions of many different subjects. 'Quodlibets' were medieval debates in which the student audience could ask 'whatever they like' (= *'quodlibet'*) of the master overseeing them.

Index

As is customary, medieval people, for whom the second name is so often a place of origin rather than a family name, are listed here by their first names; hence 'Peter Auriol', not 'Auriol, Peter'. Modern names are listed by the last name. All the book titles refer to works by Ockham. Entries marked with a * can also be found defined in the glossary.

188   *Index*

divine command morality, 27, 168
doctrine of creation, 26–27, 29,
    104–08, 110
doctrine of ten categories, 17–18
    interpretations of, 19–21
Dominic, Saint, 25

*Eight Questions on the Power of the
    Pope*, 166, 170–72
equivocation, 43–44
essence, 15–16, 20–23, 55, 57, 62–72,
    76, 79, 81–84, 97, 120, 145

fantasms, 140–43, 145–46
fictum theory of concepts, 143–45
Francis of Assisi, Saint, 25, 162, 185
Franciscan Order, 1–2, 4–5, 9, 12,
    23, 32, 134, 160, 162–65, 172
    official seal of, 1, 2, 9, 165, 173,
    175
Franciscan poverty controversy, 2, 5,
    159–170, 172
Freddoso, Alfred, 185

Gál, Gedeon, 175
Galilei, Galileo, 102
God, 23–24, 26–28, 32, 68, 82–83,
    91–94, 98, 102, 103, 132,
    149–151, 156–57, 167–68,
    170
    ability to deceive our cognitions,
    149–150
    absolute *vs.* ordained power of,
    104–110, 112, 117–18, 134,
    152, 178,
    omnipotence of, 27, 108, 110,
    178, 184

Harman, Graham, viii
Hume, David, 102

Ibn Rushd, 29

*imposition
    *first *vs.* *second, 47–53, 181–82
    use in connotative reduction, 77, 79
infinitesimal calculus, 127–28
intellectio theory of concepts,
    143–45
intention (ethics), 156–58
*intention (logic)
    *first *vs.* *second, 47–53, 181–82
    use in connotative reduction, 77
interior acts, 157–58
intuitive cognition, 145–152

Jerome, Saint, 24
Jesus, 1, 23–24, 26, 159, 161, 163,
    167–68
John Duns Scotus, 3, 35, 59, 91,
    105, 146, 157, 184
John Lutterel, 137
John of Reading, 137
John XXII, 1–2, 4–5, 8–9, 109,
    137–38, 144, 163–6,
    168–170

Kant, Immanuel, 91, 99
Keele, Lisa, viii
Kelley, Walter, 185
Kilcullen, John, 164, 171–72, 184
Kretzmann, Norman, 185

Laplace, Simon, 102
Latin language, 5, 12, 16, 24,
    27–33, 41, 43, 57–58, 62, 140,
    143–44, 166, 175, 183
Letter to the Friars Minor, 165–66,
    184
London, 2, 4, 8, 11–12, 30, 32–33,
    35–36, 41, 59, 88–89, 111–12,
    162
lordship (= *dominium*), 166–170
Louis of Bavaria, Holy Roman
    Emperor, 166, 172
Loux, Michael, 185
Luther, Martin, 109